The Reflection of Jesus, The Christ in Us

BY

Grace Black-Kimble

PUBLISHING COMPANY

The Reflection of Jesus, The Christ in Us

ISBN 978-1-946683-37-3
Library of Congress Control Number 2021916062

Rapier Publishing Company
Dothan, Alabama 36301

www.rapierpublishing.com
Facebook: www.rapierpublishing@gmail.com
Twitter: rapierpublishing@rapierpub

Book Cover Design: Garrett Myers
Book Layout: Rapture Graphics

IN THE STATE THAT I AM IN...

Presently,

The LORD inspired me in visions to implement His WORD in Biblical portraits of illustrations or parables, dissecting and conveying them into the reflection He wants us to exemplify upon the earth.

~ *Grace Black-Kimble* ~

"And we all, with unveiled face, continually seeing as in a mirror the glory of the Lord, are progressively being transformed into His image from [one degree of] glory to [even more] glory, which comes from the Lord, [who is] the Spirit."
2 Corinthians 3:18 Amplified Bible

Dedication

To my son, Dwayne Crowder, and my lovely granddaughter, Kayla Crowder, thank you for your encouragement along the way and for keeping me motivated during this journey of writing this book. Your unconditional love and support kept me in the process during moments when I felt my hope fading; your encouraging words kept me going. Continue to grow in Him spiritually as you allow His reflection, *Jesus, the Christ,* to portray in you. I love you both dearly.

Acknowledgments

Special thanks to the following individuals who were part of my spiritual journey:

Apostle, Dr. Decker Tabscott, FCCC Ministry, Warrenton, VA. Thank you for training and instructing me with my biblical studies and preparing me for ministry. I started in ministry under you, and for that, I will always be grateful.

Apostle, Senior Pastor Crosby Bonner, L.I.C., Springfield, VA., and Apostle Turnel J. Nelson, Trinidad, W.I., thank you both for officially ordaining and licensing me a Minister of the Gospel of Jesus Christ.

Apostle, Dr. Corletta J. Vaughn, Senior Pastor, Holy Ghost Cathedral Church, Detroit, MI., and Go Tell It Evangelistic Ministry, Worldwide. As my spiritual mother/ mentor, you taught and instilled in me profound spiritual revelations of God and His Kingdom. Thank you for developing and training me to become the woman of God I am today. I was your protege, and under your tutelage, I was ordained as a Minister of the Gospel of Jesus Christ on the national level from the Go Tell It Evangelistic Ministry, Worldwide. You are truly a trailblazer and forerunner among women in ministry.

Apostle Maurice K. Wright, United Christian Church, Gadsden, AL. Although you now reside in your heavenly home, you will always be my forever friend, big brother, and mentor. Your advice and guidance helped me grasp my talents and skills, becoming a better servant for God and His Kingdom.

Fannie A. Pierce, Rapier Publishing Company, Dothan, AL. You were my midwife, God's ram in the bush. You allowed the Holy Spirit to use your talents and gifts to bring forth the baby God impregnated me with for many years. Thank you for your patience, inspiration, and push. And now, *"The Reflection of Jesus, The Christ in Us,"* is birthed into the atmosphere for such a *Kairos* time as this.

Special thanks to Brenda Martin, my special friend of more than 65 years; my dear friends Apostle Teresa Smith, Brenda Wright, Apostle Diane (Frank) Cylar, and my exceptional mentors and spiritual advisors, Apostle Halton "Skip" & Pastor Alicia Horton, Day Star Tabernacle International, Douglasville, GA.

TABLE OF CONTENTS

FOREWORD

As a publisher, once in a Karios moment in time, you come across a book that you know comes straight from the Throne of God. Author Grace Black-Kimble's, "The Reflection of Jesus, The Christ In Us" is that book. When Mrs. Kimble approached me, stating she had to birth or bring forth what was in her for many years, I had no earthly concept that what she was carrying inside of her was so powerful, yet profound and simplistic, what God wanted to bring forth this season. She wanted to know if Rapier was the Publisher, God's Ram in the Bush.

Having met Mrs. Grace twenty years prior, I knew she was a mighty woman of God. I would watch her from afar, soaking in her wisdom and Godly persona. She didn't realize I was watching her, for I was the silent student who sat in the back of the room unnoticed. I admired her from my seat and never said a word but watched how she depicted what I wanted to be, a mature woman of God. Twenty years later, it wasn't by coincidence or happenchance our paths would meet again. It was a God-appointed time.

Rarely do I come across a book that will make me think and see as this book did. It changed my perspective from seeing a wedding, buying insurance, and the birth of a child. I will never view them as everyday life again. Now, I see them as God intended for me to see them in the spiritual realm, allowing me to glimpse His Dumanis power that radiates the earth.

With sincere humility, I am grateful to God for allowing Rapier to publish such a book of this caliber. I am thankful for the privilege, the opportunity, and more importantly, to Mrs. Grace, who allowed me to sit at her feet and glean her wisdom and aroma of God. Mrs. Grace stated that "I was the Ram in the Bush." However, she was the one who God used to show me His Glory in a way I have never seen.

"The Reflection of Jesus, The Christ In Us" is necessary and a must READ for the Body of CHRIST. It is time for the Body of Christ, The Bride of Christ, to reflect His image upon the earth. This book will show you the way.

God Bless
Fannie Pierce
Rapier Publishing Company

INTROUDUCTION

The Reflection of Jesus, The Christ in Us

The theological system of man's interpretation of how God operates throughout time is called dispensations. There are seven dispensations of time. According to the current timeline, we are in the Dispensation of Grace Age, sometimes called the "Age of Grace" or the "Church Age." It's the creation and expansion of the manifestation of God's Church, the Body of Christ. Although it was talked about in the Old Testament by the prophets, it started with the Resurrection of Jesus, thus the New Covenant when Christ died and rose again, defeating the enemy. The New Covenant signifies that the Law no longer binds us, but we are set free by the finished work of Jesus Christ. The Believers' sole function is to believe in the One Who He, God has sent, Jesus, The Christ. In this Age, the Holy Spirit, the Comforter, (our Paraclete) is manifested in all Believers. His purpose is to comfort and guide us to the Truth, which is the Word, making us more like the Son, Jesus.

In this powerful book, the author portrays how Jesus' reflection, His image, must be mirrored in the Body of Christ for the world to witness the manifestation of why Jesus came down to Earth. Jesus' mission was to restore us to our true identity, who we were before the fall of man. That identity was God's reflection of Himself in us. God wants Believers to demonstrate His Dunamis power of the Holy Spirit and that power to permeate throughout the world. God's power reigns in us. His reflection of who He is in each Believer. As the Church grows and matures in the sanctification process in Christ, His reflection becomes evident in our lives. When we are fully living in the fullness of

Christ, Jesus' reflection will shadow the Earth.

This book is depicted in three demonstrational elements of simplicity in the natural paralleling the spiritual of how we, the Church, should reflect Jesus on the Earth: "The Bride of Christ: The Portrait of His Bride," "The Divine Insurance Policy," and "The Womb of God Upon the Earth Through Prayer." For biblical purposes and illustrations or parables, it is designed for Believers to learn, engage, and grow, bringing the Believer to a place of maturity, becoming the man or woman God placed in the Earth to make a difference. Hopefully, after reading this book and going through the workbooks, you will see yourself as Christ sees you, comprehending the full magnitude of who you are and whom you belong to, but more importantly, you will reflect the image of God, God's reflection in you, for all to see.

PART I

The Portrait of the Bride of Christ

The Portrait of the Bride of Christ

If you ask bridal consultants, venue owners, bridal boutiques establishments, or flower shop keepers, they will tell you that June is the most sought out month for weddings. Many young ladies dream of their wedding day and being a June Bride. Marriage is a rite of passage from young girl to womanhood, becoming a wife, but a June Bride for many is a quintessential element of the passage. Whether it has been embedded in our early youthful minds by cunning advertising agencies or mass media conglomerates, it is still true today, June is the month for weddings.

For the romantic bride, it's the start of a blissful union. The weather is perfect. Spring has flung, and it's the beginning of summer as warmer days, and lazy breezes penetrate the air. The temperatures are just right. The flowers have bloomed, producing beautiful arrays of colorful bouquets cascading the Earth. not to mention the aroma of fragrance permeating the land. It's a perfect time to be a bride. The atmosphere is set, and the Earth is its stage. When the bride walks down the aisle, everybody can see the glow and joy on her face. As she walks towards her groom, he waits eagerly for his bride to come and stand by him. In his eyes, she's a beautiful reflection of the perfect bride.

In the natural how the bride prepares and gets ready for her big day is as important as the day itself. She has planned this day since she was a young girl dressing up in the mirror, humming to the tune, "Here Comes the Bride." In her preparation, she scans the Internet, bridal magazines, and brochures to find the perfect dress and shoes to match. She goes to bridal stores trying on many different dresses until she finds the one that will reflect the bride in her. She ponders over earrings. They have to be exquisite, matching the dress décor. Finally, she chooses the veil. The veil is her covering. Whether she chooses a veil to go on her head or one to cover her face, the veil portrays the final illusion of perfection. It is her covering for the groom, her soon to be husband, to uncover and see his bride for the first time.

She hires a wedding consultant or planner who will assist her in making her day special. If money is not flowing, she has family and close friends to help her. Together, they will assist her in preparing for her day. They will plan a church wedding or rent a venue to have the wedding. They will schedule the cake tasting; hire the caterers, the DJ or band, and the photographer. They schedule appointments with the manicurist to get her feet and nails done. They employ a makeup consultant to do her face and a cosmetologist to do her hair. She may need a skin specialist to make sure she has radiant and glowing skin. Blemishes, rashes, or pimples are not allowed on her special day. Her diet will change. No longer are sweets and certain foods permitted to touch her mouth. Perfection is the end goal.

She gathers her close friends and family members, and from them, she selects her bridal party, her bride maids, maid of honor, and the flower girls. She consults with the groom and they choose the best man, the ushers, and the ring bearers. She coordinates all the colors of the wedding party. The colors will match the décor of the theme and reflect the moment. Nothing is left undone, everything has been planned, and now it is finished. It is time; her wedding day is here. She is ready. Everything and everyone is in place. The consultant or family and friends are at her beck and call. The bride doesn't have to do anything on her own. On her special day, it's all about the bride. She doesn't have to worry. She only has to focus on her special day.

Once the bride is dressed, she looks into the mirror. In the mirror, she sees the reflection of who she is; she sees the bride in her. In the mirror, she sees the reflection of what she's about to do. She sees the reflection of her groom, and with one final look, she is now ready to meet her groom. The maid of honors, the bride maids, and the ushers have all proceeded before her down the aisle. The ground or carpet is arrayed with beautiful flowers. It is now time for the main event. The bride has made her entrance. She stands in the doorway. The brightest moment of the day is about to take place. The music begins to play at her arrival. Everyone stands up as she walks down the aisle. No one says a word. All eyes are on the bride and everybody appears happy and overjoyed because for that moment, they see the purity and holiness of the occasion. The groom is in the front looking at his bride as she walks down the aisle. From afar, he sees the reflection of himself in his bride. Patience has paid off. She is the personification of perfection. It is time to gather his bride.

As in the natural, as the bride prepares for her wedding day, so it is in the spiritual, as we the Body of Christ, His Church prepares for our special day, when the Groom, Jesus comes for His Bride. What a day it will be! The bride in the natural prepares for her wedding day in her dressing room. In the spiritual, the dressing room is the Earth. The bride in the natural has a group of people to assist in her preparation. Our most important Assistant or Helper is the Holy Spirit. He helps us by guiding us with His Wisdom and His Truth. He selects the best attire for us, for He knows what the Groom wants for His Bride. As with the natural groom, Jesus, our Groom, wants to see His reflection in His Bride. The Holy Spirit is the Bride's Paraclete. He prepares her for that big day. Like the natural bride trust her wedding consultant, it is vital that the Church trust in the Holy Spirit. He keeps us from tumbling and from the snares of the enemy whose goal is to attempt to stop the wedding.

The bride in the natural seeks out advice from experts, consultants, and nowadays, social media on being the perfect bride. She gathers all the information and decides what is best for her. In the spiritual, we don't seek out those factors, along with the Holy Spirit; we have God's Word to assist our preparation. We read and study His word daily. We meditate day and night on His word. As we meditate on His Word, we use our consultant, the Holy Spirit, to teach us how to operate by the word of God and allow Him to guide us in Truth, which is the word of God. We conform to the image the Groom wants, and anything contrary or opposes His image for us we take off. We take off the fruit of our labor, our self, and we put on the fullness of the Groom, the finished work of Jesus Christ.

The natural bride's dressing is adorned with everything needed to make the bride comfortable in her preparation. As so in the natural, it is in the spiritual. The earth is our dressing room until Jesus comes back for us. It is also adorned with everything we need to prepare us for our wedding day. The mirror in our dressing room allows us to see our reflection. In the beginning phases of our preparation, we don't see Jesus' Bride. We see the reflection of ourselves...our will, our desires, and worldly influences. However, as we continue to gaze into the mirror, we think of the sixty-six books of the Bible, from Genesis to Revelations. While looking through that mirror, our journey on earth, we study the sixty-six books of the Bible. The books are perfecting us to be the Bride God has called us to be. As we partake in His Word, we start to take off our reflection and put on His reflection. It's a process, so we continue to gaze into the mirror.

In this journey of preparation as the Bride of Christ, we are being restored. We are being perfected. We are becoming. Everything that needs to be taken off, He takes off. Everything we need to put on, He puts on us. If He doesn't like our attire, even if we do, He takes it off and put His garments on us. As the Bride, we don't compromise. We want the Groom to be pleased. Sometimes in the natural when a bride is getting her make-up professionally done, the specialist may apply more makeup than the bride wants. When the bride looks into the mirror, she doesn't see herself; she doesn't see the bride she wants to be. Therefore, the makeup specialist has to take off makeup and apply it again as many times as needed until the bride sees her reflection in the mirror. If the shoes, although they are pretty and match the dress, are too tight or uncomfortable to walk in, they too are discarded. A new pair is needed. For the bride, out-er beauty is essential, but the objective of the bride is to make sure that her attire from head to toe is everything she visualized for that day. When she looks into the mirror, her reflection, the bride looks back.

When we look in the mirror, as the Church, we want to see Jesus' refection; therefore, we take off everything that needs to be taken off. During this process of sanctification, we are being transformed into His image and His likeness, and our spiritual mirror, the Bible is preparing us.

As the Bride of Christ, the Church, we are in the restoration, deliverance, and transformation process. We are being restored, perfected, taking off everything that is not like Him. Jesus said in John 15: 1-2, *"I am the true grapevine, and my Father is the gardener. He cuts off every branch of mine that doesn't produce fruit, and he prunes the branches that do bear fruit so they will produce even more."* Some things in our lives will be deleted permanently; some things s will be taken off and then put back on. We may have to leave others behind. We have to get rid of self, our will, and our desires, and as we continue to gaze in the mirror, we see His Truth; it cleanses us up. It shows our blemishes, our dirt, and our disarray. We see them, and with the help of our consultant, the Holy Spirit, allow Him to do what He needs to do in our lives. It's a never-ending process until we meet our Groom.

As we prepare for Our Groom, Jesus prepares for the wedding feast with His Bride, the Church. The Church is made up of individuals, Believers who have put their trust in Jesus as their Savior, and as a result of that trust, will receive eternal life with Him. Jesus sacrificed His life to be the Savior. In Ephesians 5: 25-27, it says, *"Husbands, love your wives, just as Christ also loved the church and gave Himself for her, that He might [a]sanctify and cleanse her with the washing of water by the word, that He might present her to Himself a glorious church, not having spot or wrinkle or any such thing, but that she should be holy and without blemish."* Revelations 19: 7-9 says, *"Let us be glad and rejoice and give Him glory, for the marriage of the Lamb has come, and His wife has made herself ready." And to her it was granted to be arrayed in fine linen, clean and bright, for the fine linen is the righteous acts of the saints. Then he said to me, "Write: 'Blessed are those who are called to the marriage supper of the Lamb!'" And he said to me, "These are the true sayings of God."*

As the natural groom prepares to meet his bride, he is saying to God that he will protect and love the woman God gave him.

The Reflection of Jesus, The Christ in Us

He makes a covenant with God saying, "I take the woman, the bride as my wife. I give myself to her, protecting her, loving her as Christ loved the Church." God called the man, the husband, to love his wife and to cherish his wife, to cleanse his wife and recognize that she's the weaker vessel. Christ's relationship with the Church, as the Bride and Groom, is a replica of His relationship with the Heavenly Father. The Bride of Christ, the Church must submit to the authority of Jesus Christ and surrender her will to the will of the Groom. The husband is the head of the wife, as Christ is the Head of the Church. In the natural, the relationship between the husband and wife is a type of relationship between Christ and His Church. In the spiritual, Jesus is the perfect Groom. Jesus gave His life for His Bride. He came from Heaven to restore His Bride, and one day He will come and get His Bride. Jesus loves and cherishes His Bride. He covers and protects her. Jesus' death on the cross became a living embodiment of the Bridegroom and a faithful husband to the bride. He gave His life for His Bride so His Bride can have eternal life with Him. One day, Jesus will present His Bride to the Father as a radiant Church without stain, wrinkle, or any blood blemish but holy and blameless, restoring her back to the Father.

When the time is ready, Jesus will come back for His Bride. No one knows when Jesus will return, so we must continue to prepare for our Groom. We must continue to gaze into the mirror until we see the reflection of His Bride. *"Heaven and earth will pass away, but My words will not pass away. But no one knows the day or the hour. No! Not even the angels in heaven know. The Son does not know. Only the Father knows,"* Matthew 24: 35-37. Until then, the reflection of the Groom must be seen in us for the world. Our light must illuminate the world's darkness. We are the salt of this world. Jesus said in Matthew 5: 13-16, *"You are the salt of the earth; but if the salt loses its flavor, how shall it be seasoned? It is then good for nothing but to be thrown out and trampled underfoot by men. "You are the light of the world. A city that is set on a hill cannot be hidden. Nor do they light a lamp and put it under a basket, but on a lampstand, and it gives light to all who are in the house. Let your light so shine before men, that they may see your good works and glorify your Father in heaven."*

Jesus wants His Church to look like His Bride. He wants us to portray our light for others to see. The confidence in who we are and who we belong to is our stance. Our joy is in His strength. The world must see that although we are in the world, we do not partake in the world's way of doing things. As Jesus time was coming to an end on the Earth; He was about to go to the cross to die for our sin; He prayed to the Father (John 17) for the ones the Father gave Him. He prayed to the Father to keep us, *"They are not of the world, just as I am not of the world. Sanctify them by Your truth. Your word is truth. As You sent Me into the world, I also have sent them into the world,"* John 17: 16-18.

The portrait of Jesus' Bride is strong and mighty, pulling down strongholds, going into the enemy's camp, defeating the enemy, healing the sick and brokenhearted, and treading on serpents and scorpions. When Jesus rose, He rose with all power, Dunamis power, the power of God. God gave this power to Believers to live devotional, pure and holy lives until He returns for us. The word Dunamis means power, force, and/, ability. In 2 Timothy 1:7, it says, *"For God gave us not a spirit of fear, but of power, love and self-control.."* This power He gave us was His. We have God's power to reflect His Bride while we are still on Earth.

In this power, we have the fullness of Christ and His full armor. To live in this world, the Bride of Christ must put on

God's full armor. God's armor keeps us from being deceived, enticed, and fooled by the devil's schemes and maneuvers. The Bible says we must not be ignorant of Satan's devices (2 Corinthians 2:11). It also says in John 10:10, "*The thief does not come except to steal, and to kill, and to destroy. I have (Jesus) come that they may have life, and that they may have it more abundantly.*" Satan will do anything and everything to keep us from looking like the Bride of Christ. His mission is to try to stop as many from portraying Jesus's Bride. The power is in the fullness of Christ and the full of armor of God. God's Holy Spirit keeps us from portraying anything other than the Bride of Christ. That's why we keep gazing into the mirror, taking off everything that doesn't look like a bride. We keep our focus on the wedding day.

The natural bride doesn't allow anything or anyone to stop her special day. The only thing she can visualize is walking down the aisle to meet her groom. From the day she said yes, nothing else matters. Her wedding day takes precedence. Her attire is her armor. She puts on the armor that portrays her as the bride. When the natural bride walks down the aisle everybody will know that she's the bride. Her light is radiant and glowing. She is adorned in white, and her radiance shows her faith in the marriage covenant. Her reflection portrays she is the bride. Her full armor is on; the dress and shoes, the earrings, the veil, and the bouquet. Her attire tells everyone she has prepared for this day. When she walks down the aisle with her full armor on, she depicts she is ready for the next step in her life. She is prepared to be a wife. She is ready for her husband. Nothing is left to do; everything that didn't go with the presentation was discarded. The months, weeks, days, and hours in preparation were worth the wait. Here comes the bride.

The Armor of the Natural Bride:

The wedding dress is the emblem of purity and innocence. It represents the end of childhood, the end of adolescence, and the beginning of womanhood. The bride yields to her chosen one in full commitment to him and only him, thus uniting two into one. The wedding dress is carefully thought of, selected, and fitted to match the bride's reflection. When the groom sees her, he remembers the day that he chose her to be his bride.

The veil covers the bride's face or head. In ancient times, brides wore veils to depict obedience and modesty, especially in ancient religious cultures, where veils were seen as a symbol of reverence for women to cover their heads. In early Rome, women wore veils to keep away evil spirits so nothing could ruin the bride's joy. Typically, the veil is worn as a covering of respect and honor to the reverence of the day. Sometimes, the veil is uncovered by the bride's father; other times, the Groom lifts the veil, revealing his bride for the first time. The veil is the bride's glory on her head.

The wedding bouquet is just as significant to the wedding dress. It's essential to today's bridal attire. The bouquet brings out the essence of the dress and adds elegance and beauty to the bride's demeanor as she walks down the aisle. Many believe the bouquet will bring happiness and bloom to marriage. In ancient times, the bride carried or wore flowers garlands, believing they signified a new beginning, fidelity, and fertility. It was during the Victorian age that flowers bouquet became official. The bride chooses the bouquet representing her sentiment for the day and what she wants to bloom for the marriage.

The wedding shoes can't be seen as the bride walks the aisle, but without good comfort and style, not having proper shoes can put a damper on the bride's day.

You may wonder why it is necessary to reflect in such detail about the natural bride. To understand the role of the Church as Jesus Bride, one must understand the role of the natural bride. The bride prepares for her wedding day. The moment she is betrothed, the planning is in full effect. No longer will she think of anything else; her entire thought process is on her wedding day. Her wedding day is one of the most significant days in her life. For the Body of Christ, the Church, we are the Bride of Christ. The moment we become saved and accept Jesus as our Lord and Savior, just like the natural bride, we should be preparing for our spiritual wedding. Although some readers may say that this is not a book about brides, it is profitable that you understand the significance of both. One is in the natural, the other spiritual. Both are important aspects to the bride; however, one is an earthly perspective, the other is heavenly gain. Many Believers understand the natural bride preparation for her wedding day, but when dealing with the Bride of Christ preparation for the Groom for our wedding day, we failed to grasp the magnitude of that day. Although they correlate to a degree, they are very different. If you can see how the natural bride is parallel to the spiritual Bride, you will see how we as the Church need to prepare for our Wedding.

In the spiritual, we too must put on the full armor of God as the Bride of Christ, His Portrait, and the portrait of God. When the world sees us, it will see the full armor of the Bride on. When we walk down the aisle, Jesus will see that we have the breastplate of righteousness, His righteousness on. On our head is the helmet of salvation. In our hands is the Shield of Faith. The Belt of Truth is our under coverings. The radiant glow represents the Sword of the Spirit. And our shoes are made of peace. The enemy can't touch us because our Shield and Sword protect us from his fiery arrows. We are glowing because we are covered by the finished work of Jesus Christ and the power of the Holy Spirit.

"Finally, my brethren, be strong in the Lord and in the power of His might. 11 Put on the whole armor of God, that you may be able to stand against the [b]wiles of the devil. 12 For we do not wrestle against flesh and blood, but against principalities, against powers, against the rulers of [c]the darkness of this age, against spiritual hosts of wickedness in the heavenly places. 13 Therefore take up the whole armor of God that you may be able to withstand in the evil day, and having done all, to stand. Stand therefore, having girded your waist with truth, having put on the breastplate of righteousness, 15 and having shod your feet with the preparation of the gospel of peace; 16 above all, taking the shield of faith with which you will be able to quench all the fiery darts of the wicked one. 17 And take the helmet of salvation, and the sword of the Spirit, which is the word of God," Ephesians 6: 10-17.

As you gaze into the spiritual mirror and prepare to dress for the wedding, as the Bride of Christ, you must put on the Full Armor of God:

You Must Put On: <u>The Belt of Truth</u>:

When we look in the mirror, we need the Belt of Truth. The Belt of Truth is the first piece of Amor we must put on. Without the Truth of God's word we are lost. Without the Belt of Truth, we can't put on the rest of the armor because we won't know Truth to make us free (*"And ye shall know the truth, and the truth shall make you free,"* John 8:32.) It is a crucial armor in our defense against Satan. It protects and prepares us for battle. Satan is the father of lies so deception is high on his list. We put on God's Truth to resist Satan and not succumb to his lies and deception. When we have the Belt of Truth around our waist us as armor, when Satan comes and tries to deceive us, we have the word of God as the truth. Satan came to deceive Jesus in the wilderness after Jesus had fasted for forty days and nights. However, because Jesus knew the Truth, God's Word, He said to Satan, *"It is written...,"* (Luke 4: 1-13). Satan couldn't deceive or entice Jesus because Jesus knew the Truth. So it is with us. When we know the Truth, the enemy can't fool us or tempt us with worldly pleasures.

A belt is designed to keep your pants from falling down. It is the same with the Belt of Truth; it keeps us from falling into the enemy's traps and schemes when we wear it. When we wear His Truth we believe the word of God over Satan lies. As a result, nothing will fall down or get us off course or distracted. We don't compromise because we know the Truth. The Belt of Truth serves as our foundation. As the Bride of Christ, when we put on His Truth, we look more like Jesus. When we have His Truth girded firmly around our waist, we can stand the wiles of the enemy. It protects us until we meet our Groom.

You Must Put On: <u>The Breastplate of Righteousness</u>:

The second pierce of armor we put on is the Breastplate of Righteousness. This piece of armor is to guard our hearts. The heart is a vital organ; if pierced in the natural, the result is immediate death, so in the natural, so in the spiritual. We put on God's righteousness to keep from deceiving ourselves.

Jeremiah 17:9 says, *"The heart is deceitful above all things, and desperately wicked: who can know it?"* The righteousness of God keeps us from our own deception of thinking we are more than what we are and who we are. His Righteousness keeps us from deceiving ourselves it's in our strength and might, for the word says in Zachariah 4:6, *"This is the word of the LORD to Zerubbabel: 'Not by might nor by power, but by My Spirit....'"* God's righteousness is not in our ability but in the ability of the finished work of Jesus Christ. It is in His righteousness we are righteous and not because of ourselves. Therefore the Breastplate of Righteousness keeps us humbled, lowly, and full of meekness. It keeps us from being proud. It gives us a tender heart for others, as God the Father has a tender heart for us. It shows no favoritism, no respecter of person. It allows us to love our neighbors as we love ourselves. His Righteousness keeps our focus on the things of God. When we wear the Breastplate of Righteousness, our hearts become more pure, sanctified, and we are being conformed into the image of Christ. We submit to His authority, His will and allow the Holy Spirit to teach us God's Truth. We are seeking God's way of doing things…His Righteousness above our way and thoughts.

"For My thoughts are not your thoughts, Nor are your ways My ways," says the LORD. "For as the heavens are higher than the earth, So are My ways higher than your ways, And My thoughts than your thoughts," Isaiah 55:8-9.

God's Righteousness is a gift; it cannot be earned, so we put it on knowing it is a gift from our Heavenly Father. When we put on the Breastplate of Righteousness, we are right with God, not in our doing but in Christ. Therefore when the Father sees us, He doesn't see us. He sees His Son.

You Must Take Up: <u>The Shield of Faith:</u>

The Shield of Faith is the piece of armor we used to protect us from the enemy's fiery darts. The Shield of Faith covers our body; it provides a blanket of protection. When the enemy comes in, we have to take up our Shield. In Genesis 15:1, the LORD told Abram that He was Abram's Shield: "After these things the word of the LORD came to Abram in a vision, saying, *Do not be afraid, Abram. I am your shield, your exceedingly great reward."* We take up the Shield of Faith, causing our faith to be in God's Word and His promises. When we have faith in God and His Word, we can stand against the penetrating flames of Satan. The Shield of Faith provides full protection from Satan's attacks. The Lord is our Shield, our Groom, and therefore, no weapon will prosper against us. How do we take up the Shield of Faith? By believing and keep believing God's Word. The more faith we have, the more protection and power the Shield is to intercept attacks. (Flaming arrows of the evil one Ephesians 6:16.)

A shield is essential to any soldier. Hebrew 11:1, *"Now faith is confidence in what we hope for and assurance about us do not see."* Without faith it is impossible to please God. Satan attacks can sometimes make us doubt God, but our Shield keeps us from doubting; it gives us hope in Him and His Word. We have to deliberately choose to have faith in God in all circumstances. Faith is not blind belief; it's a solid belief in the One Sent. Faith reminds us of God's promises in His Word. Faith is the protected barrier between the Believer and Satan. We keep our Shield on at all times.

You Must Put On: <u>The Helmet of Salvation:</u>

The bride in the natural has a veil on her head. It's her covering. In the spiritual our head covering is the Helmet of Salvation. For the Believer, it protects us from what goes into our mind. The mind is a battlefield. When we put on the Helmet of Salvation, we are putting on the Word of God; thus, the Word is penetrating our mind, resulting in having the mind of Christ. Therefore, when we put on the Helmet of Salvation, we are putting on the mind of Christ. The Word is a mind regulator. It regulates our mind, and anything contrary to God's Word, we don't receive it. That's why believers need to study and meditate in His Word day and night. The Helmet of Salvation is the head seat of the mind. When we know the Truth, we don't receive false doctrines. No one can deceive us as we keep the Helmet of Salvation on as our head covering. The Helmet protects the head, our thoughts, our emotions, and our feelings. Without the Helmet, we leave ourselves exposed on the battlefield; the enemy can beguile us as he did with Eve, resulting in a damaged or confused mind. When this happens, the rest of the armor will have no effect.

We renew our minds daily with the Word of God. We don't listen to the deceptions of the enemy. We don't doubt what God says. The enemy wants us to focus on what's happening in the world, the world's system, and the world's way of doing things. He wants us to focus on the many plagues, the injustices, the famines, and the evils that demand our attention. We need to know these things and have compassion, but not allow these things to take our focus off the Truth and God's promises. When we take off the Helmet of Salvation and become entangled in the world's way, we allow ourselves to doubt what God says. Our doubt can turn into mistrust, disobedience, and backsliding. Jesus came to save us from our sins and to restore us to our original identity. The Helmet of Salvation continues to save us from the snares of the enemy and keeps us safe on the battlefield until Jesus comes back. The more we put on the Helmet of Salvation, the more our minds will become like the mind of Christ. And no longer will Satan be able to influence us with worldly thoughts, traps, lusts, and desires.

You Must Take Up: <u>The Sword of the Spirit</u>:

The Sword of the Spirit is the Word of God. When we are tempted, the most effective weapon that God has given us is His Word. It is the only weapon God gave us as an actual armor fighting weapon against the enemy. The Sword of the Spirit belongs to the Holy Spirit. The Holy Spirit is both our defensive and offensive weapon when fighting Satan. God refers to His Word as a sword, Hebrews 4:12, *"For the word of God is living and powerful, and sharper than any two-edged sword, piercing even to the division of soul and spirit, and of joints and marrow, and is a discerner of the thoughts and intents of the heart."* The sword represents the power of God to fight the influence of evil and change people's lives. It has the power to free people from strongholds and demonic spirits. The Belt of Truth we are learning it, whereas the Sword of the Spirit, we are practicing it. When we know the Word of God, we use our Sword to penetrate the enemy's camp, free people from captivity, tread on scorpions, and heal the sick and brokenhearted. The Holy Spirit is our Sword...the Word of God. Jesus said in John 14: 26, *"But the Helper, the Holy Spirit, whom the Father will send in My name, He will teach you all things, and bring to your remembrance all things that I said to you."* The Holy Spirit teaches us how to use the Sword, the Word. He trains us with the Word. The purpose of the Sword of the Spirit is to make us strong in God's power and to fight the good fight of faith. The more we know the Word, the more we can fight and stand our ground, using our Sword. The Sword of the Spirit is the holiness and power of the Word. The more we use the Sword of the Spirit, the more mature and effective we will be in doing God's will on the Earth while standing against the enemy.

You Must Put On: <u>The Shoes of Peace:</u>

Until Jesus comes back, we are in a battle. The enemy, Satan, wants us to look like the world and not the Church, the Bride of Christ. His sole mission is to keep us angry, frustrated, upset, divided, and full of strife. He doesn't want us to mirror the image of Christ. He does not have the power to keep us from eternal life, but if he can keep us from reflecting Jesus' Light on Earth, he is satisfied. The Shoes of Peace is the last piece of armor God wants us to put on. Wherever we go, we should reflect God's Peace. His Peace surpassing all understanding (Philippians 4:7). Before Jesus left, He gave us His Peace: *"Peace I leave with you, My peace I give to you; not as the world gives do I give to you. Let not your heart be troubled, neither let it be afraid,"* John 14:27. God says wherever you go in your Christian journey, go in Peace.

We put on the Shoes of Peace as we walk out our on salvation. On this earth we are in warfare; were in a war; however, although we are in a war, we have already won. The battle is not ours; it's the Lord's, and because it's the Lord's, the battle or war is won. Can you imagine going to war knowing that you have already won. Your confidence soars as you fight the enemy because no matter what happens, you've won. That's how we have to see our time on Earth as we prepare for our Groom. We won. The Shoes of Peace is the Good News. Yes, we are in battle, but since we won, we continue to share God's Word without ceasing, regardless of what we are going through or what we see. We don't put our eyes on the seen (the natural), but the unseen, the wedding reception. When we put on the Shoes of Peace, we allow the Holy Spirit to lead and guide us. He orders our steps (Psalm

119:133). We represent the Fruit of the Spirit: love, peace, joy, long-suffering, faithfulness, kindness, gentleness, goodness, and self-control. We love one another as Christ loves the Church. When we put on the Shoes of Peace on the battleground, we walk in humility and love. Our humility and love win others to Christ. There is no backbiting, jealousy, envy, or strife. In peace, we see our brother's faults, sins, but we don't judge them. We love them, showing them the way to salvation. We walk in God's grace, His power, and strength. Our Shoes enable us to turn the other cheek, forgive, and be long-suffering.

As we put on the last piece of armor, the Shoes of Peace, we will finally see the reflection of Christ's Bride, the Church, when we look into the mirror.

When Jesus comes back for His Bride, He's looking for His perfect Bride. When the Church sees the reflection of her Groom in the mirror, Jesus is ready for His Bride. When Jesus, the Christ comes, as the Groom for His Bride, He stands as she comes to the door. He sees His reflection in His Bride. He sees the portrait of His Bride. His Bride doesn't have any spot or wrinkle or any such thing; she is holy and without blemish. At the wedding feast, the Bride is arrayed in fine linen, clean and bright, for the fine linen is the righteous acts of the saints. She is sanctified and cleansed with the washing water by the Word of God. She is adorned for her Husband, the Groom, Jesus (Revelation 21:2). She has the Full Armor of God on. She is prepared to meet her Groom. *"Thy Maker is you Husband...,"* Isaiah 54:5.

Jesus' Bride, the Church, will be reunited with Christ forever. There will be a huge wedding reception, and then Jesus, our Groom, will take His Bride's hand, and together they will walk, and then with a radiant smile never seen, He will present His Bride to the Father. Until that day, we will wear our Bridal attire as we continue on the journey, allowing the sixty-six books of the Bible to show us His reflection in the mirror of His Word. As the Holy Spirit continues to consult, prepare and prune us for our wedding day.

PART II

The Divine Insurance Policy

The Divine Insurance Policy

In the natural, insurance policies protect people and their possessions from certain elements, such as natural disasters, health-related illnesses, home improvements, repairs or damages, or vehicle malfunctions or accidents. These policies provide coverage to people and their assets and are vital in creating solid foundations for one's security and sense of peace. But what is insurance? *Wikipedia defines insurance as a means of protection from financial loss. It is a form of risk management, primarily used to hedge against the risk of a contingent or uncertain loss.*[1]

There is a wide range of insurance policies intended to safeguard certain aspects of your health and assets. The most common and sought after are life insurance, health insurance, homeowners' insurance, vehicle insurance, and now due to an increased number of health issues, long-term disability insurance. Although there are more to choose from, these are the most prevalent.

1. Life insurance protects your loved ones who are financially dependent on you if something should happen to you. It is designed to ease the financial burden for your loved ones: spouse, children, parents, or other relatives and friends and provide financial security in the event of your death. People purchase life insurance policies to ease financial burdens and funeral expenses.

---

1. *https://en.wikipedia.org/wiki/Insurance*

2. Health Insurance provides coverage to cover medical expenses in the event of an illness, surgery, or routine doctor visits and general medical examinations. It also provides prescription drug and dental coverage. With the rising cost of medical care, people are making sure they have health insurance to assist with the burdens and costs.

3. Homeowner's Insurance provides coverage to repair or rebuild your home in the event of a natural disaster, such as fire, theft, vandalism, weather related damages, loss or damage of personal assets, or injury that takes place on your property. Homeowner's insurance was established to protect the overall structure, interior, and exterior of your property and ease the financial burden of rebuilding or repairing it on your own. It is important that if you own a home, you should have this coverage.

4. Automobile Insurance is the same as homeowners' insurance, but it protects your vehicle(s) instead of a home. It is designed to cover damages or theft to your vehicles and protect you financially if you are liable for another person's injuries or damages. It provides liability coverage for you and another person in case of an accident. If you have a car, you need automobile insurance.

5. Long-Term Disability Insurance covers and protects an employee from loss of income in the event he cannot work due to an illness or injury. It is to offset possible financial burdens during his time from work. Although the person may not get his full salary, getting some of his salary will ease his financial burdens until he can work again. The average length of this coverage is up to three years.

Insurance coverage is the amount of risk or liability covered for an individual or entity through insurance services. Insurance coverage, such as auto insurance, is issued by an insurer in the event of an unforeseen event. When there is an incident or unforeseen occurrence, such as a car accident, or a health-related illness, the insured person, because he has coverage, gets the support he needs. Insurance policies are broken down into premiums. The type of premium you purchase will determine the type of coverage you have, full or partial. Also, the kind of coverage you need will determine the coverage cost. A person has to pay a fee for the coverage he desires, what's best for him and/his family. Of course, if you are single, you wouldn't need family coverage, but if you have a family, you definitely would want full family coverage. If you live in an apartment, you need renter's insurance, but not home insurance. Your coverage depends on your needs and your risks factors. You pay the insurance company a monthly fee, or yearly, depending on how your plan is set up. They, in return, allocate your money to make sure that what you are insuring is covered. In the event of something happening, you contact the company, and based on your policy, the company takes care of the matter. It's not free, but in the event of a calamity or a natural disaster, it's one thing you don't have to worry about because you paid the cost of the coverage.

When shopping or selecting insurance, one must find the policy based on the needs and not wants. When one is selected, two entities are involved, the insurer and the insured. The insured person receives a contract stating all the details and specifications of the policy of the area that is to be insured. It provides the conditions and circumstances under which the insurer will compensate the insurer. The details are specified based on the type of policy and premium selected. Anything that happens outside of the policy is not deemed to be compensated. For instance, if you are smoking in bed and cause your house to catch on fire, and it was found out that it was negligence on your part, your home will not be covered. The insuring agency is not responsible for your negligence. It was specified in the contract. Therefore, you cannot demand compensation.

Most people shop for insurance carefully, and they need to; after all, they need to get the best policy for their needs and stability, not to mention peace of mind. Knowing your house is fully covered in the event of an earthquake or hurricane can cause a sense of relief in an already chaotic surrounding. Policies come in various features and boast different benefits, advantages, and costs, so it is good for you to do your due diligence when shopping for the one that best fits your needs and READ THE FINE PRINT. However, no matter what your need is, no policy has the full guarantee that it will meet all of your needs and cover all of your costs. They cannot guarantee this, and that's why there is always a fine print. No company can provide everything for you. Their job is to provide the best they can at the least effective cost for them and you. They cannot offer you a divine insurance policy.

This brings us to the second element of His Reflection of Us in Him, the subject of this section, "The Divine Insurance Policy." In the natural, just like the natural bride, when it comes to insurance, we based our security and our reflection of peace on what we see in the mirror, our reflection of man's. We purchase insurance based on what we see we need or feel we need. We base our security on a policy that provides us with false security or peace of mind, and not understanding it cannot give us total peace of mind or full divine assistance. We purchase coverage, sometimes more pricey than others, because they cover more. Some of us can afford to, whereas some cannot. Therefore, for some, we get a policy that provides adequate coverage. Hey, some coverage is better than no coverage!

It is our natural man's makeup, intelligence, and wisdom to gather information based on our capability to grasp what we deem important or vital. We look at the natural and tend to focus on what we see in the natural. Second Corinthians 4:18 tells us that, *"The things which are seen are temporal; but the things which are not seen are eternal."* In the natural, it appears that it is solid, and it gives us a sense of smug satisfaction that we have created something tangible that works. We are carefully programed to believe that getting insurance is what we need to secure our peace or stablity in the event of an unforeseen occurrence. It is subliminally forced into our mindset by advertising agencies and world financial systems. Please don't be misconstrued. I am not conveying that you don't need insurance. You do! Insurance is necessary, and you should get insurance for your possessions and for yourself. However, we need more than man-made, created policies to keep us totally safe and secure.

In the natural, if your house catches on fire, yes, home insurance provides the coverage to rebuild, giving you a sense of relief. So, yes, insurance is necessary. However, in the natural, insurance policies cover our homes, cars, possessions and assets, but heavenly insurance covers and saves our soul. It gives us a peace that passes all understanding. (*"...and the peace of God, which surpasses all understanding, will guard your hearts and minds through Christ Jesus,"* Philippians 4:7). For the Believer, we need to grasp that in the spiritual realm, we have a divine insurance policy that is PAID In Full, and the benefits are 100% covered. There are no acts of God provisions. Nothing is lacking. It was already purchased for us in full when we accepted Jesus as our Lord and Savior.

When Jesus was about to depart this earth, He gathered His disciples and informed them several things. He told them He had to leave. In fact, He stated it would be beneficial if He did leave, that's when He, the Comforter, the Holy Spirit would come: *"If you love Me, keep My commandments. And I will pray the Father, and He will give you another Helper, that He may abide with you forever— the Spirit of truth, whom the world cannot receive, because it neither sees Him nor knows Him; but you know Him, for He dwells with you and will be in you. I will not leave you orphans; I will come to you,"* John 14: 15-18. When He comes, He will show and tell you all things concerning me: *"But the Helper, the Holy Spirit, whom the Father will send in My name, He will teach you all things, and bring to your remembrance all things that I said to you,"* John 14:26. Jesus was telling them that the Holy Spirit will lead them to the Truth, and in that Truth, they will see His reflection and His divine insurance policy. Jesus told His disciples that He would never leave or forsake them. For He, Himself said, *"…I will never leave you nor forsake you,"* Hebrews 13:5. Today, Jesus continues to tell His disciples, the Church, that He will never leave us or forsake us, no matter what. If the house burns down, a loved one passes away; through sickness, disease, or illness, Jesus is always here with us. And the good news, He left us with a divine insurance policy that never has to be paid again. His coverage is everlasting and for eternity. We only have to read the contract or policy to know what we have in His coverage.

We already stated that in the natural an insurance policy is a contract between two entities, the insured and the insurer. In the contract are all the necessary wording and features of coverages. Based on the ramifications of the contractual agreements, it defines what the insured has to pay to continue to have full coverage per contract stipulations and what the insurer promises and is bound to do if there is a need. Both parties, especially the insured, need to read the contract carefully. If not, when a need arises, the insured may believe it was covered only to find out it wasn't and that it would have been covered at an additional cost. In the spiritual, once you become saved, the contract is never changing and permanently binding. However, just like in the natural, in the spiritual, if you don't know what you have covered or access to, you may walk around believing you are not covered or only partially covered.

In Ephesians 1:13-14, it says, *"In Him you also trusted, after you heard the word of truth, the gospel of your salvation; in whom also, having believed, you were sealed with the Holy Spirit of promise, who is the guarantee of our inheritance until the redemption of the purchased possession, to the praise of His glory."*

Jesus didn't leave us comfortless; Jesus told us that the Holy Spirit, the Comforter, was coming when He left. Jesus left us with a Divine Insurance Policy, and that policy was the Holy Spirit. The Holy Spirit came on earth to protect us, keep us, and guard us. He came on earth to make sure we are okay until Jesus comes back for us. His assignment is to cover us and watch over us, just like He did in the beginning when He hovered over the earth's waters (*"...and the Spirit of God was hovering over the face of the waters,"* Genesis 1). The Holy Spirit moved, protected, and created the non-existence into existence, the inorganic into the organic. The Holy Spirit is still hovering over the earth, protecting and watching over us, but now He resides in us, the Believer.

Throughout the Bible, God's Word tells us God's plans for His people. When we read His plans, it gives us a sense of security and assurance, and that is when we become saved, God has us and will continue to keep us. The assurance of God's protection can be summed up in one of the most prolific passages of scriptures in the Bible. Here, God defines His divine insurance plan for the Church. In His plan, it provides coverage, full access, and benefits for the Believer.

As Believers, our divine insurance policy is specified in Psalm 91. If we can grasp the contents of what we have, the FULL ACCESS OF JESUS CHRIST, why He came down to earth and died and rose for us, the world we see His reflection in us. In this plan, the world doesn't see us, it sees God:

"This psalm is one of the greatest possessions of the saints." (G. Campbell Morgan).²

"In the whole collection there is not a more cheering Psalm, its tone is elevated and sustained throughout, faith is at its best, and speaks nobly." (Charles Spurgeon) *"It is one of the most excellent works of this kind which has ever appeared. It is impossible to imagine anything more solid, more beautiful, more profound, or more ornamented." (de Muis, cited in Spurgeon)* ³

Psalm 91

"He who dwells in the secret place of the Most High Shall abide under the shadow of the Almighty.2 I will say of the Lord, "He is my refuge and my fortress; My God, in Him I will trust." 3 Surely He shall deliver you from the snare of the fowler And from the perilous pestilence.4 He shall cover you with His feathers, And under His wings you shall take refuge; His truth shall be your shield and buckler. 5 You shall not be afraid of the terror by night, Nor of the <u>arrow that flies</u> by day, 6 Nor of the pestilence that walks in dark-

2./3. *https://enduringword.com/bible-commentary/psalm-91/*

ness, Nor of the destruction that lays waste at noonday. 7 A thousand may fall at your side, And ten thousand at your right hand; But it shall not come near you. 8 Only with your eyes shall you look, And see the reward of the wicked. 9 Because you have made the Lord, who is my refuge, Even the Most High, your dwelling place, 10 No evil shall befall you, Nor shall any plague come near your dwelling; 11 For He shall give His angels charge over you, To keep you in all your ways. 12 In their hands they shall bear you up, Lest you dash your foot against a stone. 13 You shall tread upon the lion and the cobra, The young lion and the serpent you shall trample underfoot. 14 "Because he has set his love upon Me, therefore I will deliver him; I will set him on high, because he has known My name. 15 He shall call upon Me, and I will answer him; I will be with him in trouble; I will deliver him and honor him.16 With long life I will satisfy him And show him My salvation."

When Jesus departed the earth to be with the Father, He made sure He took care of His new family. Jesus prayed to the Father for Him to keep us:

"I pray for them. I do not pray for the world but for those whom You have given Me, for they are Yours. And all Mine are Yours, and Yours are Mine, and I am glorified in them. Now I am no longer in the world, but these are in the world, and I come to You. Holy Father, keep through Your name those whom You have given Me, that they may be one as We are. While I was with them]in the world, I kept them in Your name. Those whom You gave Me I have kept; and none of them is lost except the son of [h]perdition, that the Scripture might be fulfilled," John 17: 9-12.

"I do not pray that You should take them out of the world, but that You should keep them from the evil one. They are not of the world, just as I am not of the world," John 17: 15-16.

The Reflection of Jesus, The Christ in Us

In Psalm 91, God's divine contract for us specifies everything Jesus asked the Father to do before He departed. It specifies what the policy entails, the stipulations, and the specifications. It depicts who Jesus said God is when He was on earth, and most importantly, how much He loves His children. The highlights of the plan are:

1. God is our Refuge and Fortress.
2. God will deliver us from snares of the Fowler.
3. God is a covering.
4. You will not fear the terror at night nor day.
5. You will not fear pestilence or destruction
6. Others may fall around you, but you will not be touched.
7. No evil shall befall you.
8. No plague shall come to your house.
9. Angels will watch over you.
10. You will tread and trample over evil.
11. God will hear you and rescue you when you call out to Him.
12. God will give you a satisfied, long life and show you His salvation.

No natural insurance company can guarantee these things; only God can. His insurance policy covers everything we need. It covers diseases, sicknesses, protection from the seen and unseen, plagues, calamities, it provides deliverance and healing, whatever there is a need of, God's divine insurance policy covers that need. If we can see what we have in the spiritual is far greater than the policies we have in the natural, knowing that we are fully covered, we would be a people that would portray His reflection on earth. Regardless of the storms or calamities, our light will shine, penetrating the darkness for the blind to see. The rain will descend on the saved and the unsaved, "... *for He makes His sun rise on the evil and on the good, and sends rain on the just and on the unjust,"* Matthew 5:45; evil will arise because we are in the world, but it will not overtake us; destruction will come, but because we have a divine insurance policy with God, we are one-hundred percent covered. Jesus's Blood paid the premium in full. In Jesus, we have life insurance, house insurance, auto insurance, business insurance, flood insurance, and long-term disability insurance. When we depart this earth, we are with Him in the twinkling of an eye. So although illnesses or diseases may come, we have a full assurance that we will be with Him forever in eternity.

Unfortunately, we don't know the full impact of what we have if we don't read or understand the contents of our divine policy. Just like there are stipulations in a natural policy, there are stipulations in our divine insurance policy. It is not guaranteed until we meet the criteria. And the only true criterion of the policy is that we must dwell in the secret place of the Most High God. The blessings and promises in this policy are designed for all Believers; however, all Believers will not receive the fullness of the policy. To receive the fullness, you have to abide in the secret place; live in close fellowship with God. That is the condition.

"The first and only true stipulation of our insurance policy is to dwell in the secret place of the Most High, El Elyon."

<u>"He who dwells in the secret place of the Most High Shall abide under the shadow of the Almighty."</u>

God's secret place is hidden. You have to seek the LORD, Creator of heaven and earth and dwell (live) in His presence, El Shadday.

Most High – in Hebrew, it is Elyon. It means lofty, elevation, and supreme. Most High denotes God's supreme authority over all other authorities. Almighty – in Hebrew, it is Shadday. It means most powerful, denoting that there is no power greater than God in the vast universe. LORD – in Hebrew, it is written as YHWH, pronounced as Yahweh. which literally means the Self-Existent or Eternal One. The name Yahweh itself implies the eternal nature of God. He is outside the physical realm. He is not limited by time, space, and matter! Yahweh has neither beginning nor end. God – came from the Hebrew word, Elohim. It basically means God. You have to dwell in God.[4]

The word dwell means to live in or at a specified place. It says, *"He that dwells."* The person or Believer, has to live in a specified place, and this place is in the secret place of the Most High. When we dwell in the secret place, there are promises of safety, provisions, security, and favor. To dwell you must:

- Set your priority on Him.
- Continuously seek His Presence.
- Humble yourself before Him.
- Surrender your will and your life for His will and His plans for you.

God wants to have an intimate relationship with His children. We were created to have fellowship with God. In the Secret Place intimacy occurs. In this place of dwelling, intimate conversation and fellowship between you and God take place. In this place, you are becoming one with God, allowing Him to be your God in and over all things pertaining to your life, including you, your will, and your desires. When we are living in the secret place of God, God shows us His covenant. We

4. *https://becomingchristians.com/2018/02/26/20-most-surprising-lessons-from-psalm-91-you-probably-never-heard-of/*

cannot claim all of Psalm 91 promises if we do not dwell in the SHELTER of the <u>Most</u> <u>High.</u> We may have partial coverage but not 100% coverage.

"The secret of the Lord is with them that fear him; and he will shew them his covenant," Psalm 25:14.

This passage does not indicate fear in the natural, whereas it brings torture or bad news, but fear in regards to humbling ourselves with humility, honor, respect, and reverence. Reverence means deep respect and honor for someone or something. When we reverence and honor God for who He is, God shows Himself to us. In this setting of humility, God is able to guide and instruct us in the paths that He desires or planned for us to go. The secret place is total trust and surrender of our will.

God wants us to dwell in Him so that He can show His fullness to us. It is no different than in the times of Moses. The LORD told Moses to build Him a tabernacle, a dwelling place so He can reside with His people. He gave Moses specific, detailed instructions on how He wanted it to be built. The tabernacle was God's Shekinah Glory and denoted the divine presence of God. Today, the dwelling place, the tabernacle of God, is in the Believer's heart. When we dwell in the secret place of The Most High, God's Shekinah glory will permeate our lives and saturate the earth.

Jesus understood the secret place in God. Jesus said in John 6:38-40, *"For I have come down from heaven, not to do My own will, but the will of Him who sent Me. This is the will of the Father who sent Me, that of all He has given Me I should lose nothing, but should raise it up at the last day. And this is the will of Him who sent Me, that everyone who sees the Son and believes in Him may have everlasting life; and I will raise him up at the last day."* Jesus didn't have an earthly agenda but a heavenly assignment. Jesus was able to finish His assignment because He dwelled in the presence of God; He lived in God. We have to live and dwell in God's secret place to get the fullness of His divine insurance policy. This secret place is our home, our habitation. If we do not seek or dwell in this place, we cannot receive the fullness of His divine protection.

To receive 100% full coverage, we must adhere to the all-inclusive policy. We cannot do the partial and expect full benefits. It doesn't work that way in the natural, and it doesn't work that way in the spiritual. We can't look towards the inner sanctuary and the mercy seat and not dwell permanently there. Yes, we run to it at times when there are problems, and we enjoy occasional approaches, but not to habitually reside in the secret place of God is to forfeit our full coverage and benefits of His plan. To not dwell permanently is to forfeit what Jesus prayed for us. In the secret place, those who dwell in this place lives are changed into the full manifestation of Christ. The Believer who seeks and lives there, the veil is torn, the mercy seat is revealed, the covering cherubs are manifested, and the glory of the Most High is present. In this setting, the presence of God, His throne, is a place of divine access, communion, and propitiation for all who desire to abide in.

When you abide by the first and only stipulation of the policy, you can gain full access to God's Divine Insurance Plan. You can say:

<u>"He is my refuge and my fortress; My God, in Him I will trust."</u>
<u>(Verse 2)</u>

The word refuge means a condition of being safe or sheltered from pursuit, danger, or trouble. You are saying, LORD, you are my safety, my shelter, my protection. The word fortress means a fortified stronghold, a military defense protection. When you dwell and abide in the LORD, He becomes your refuge in times of duress and trouble, building a fortified wall around you, sheltering you from anything or anyone that seeks to hurt, harm, or destroy you. In this fortified place, nothing can penetrate its walls; it cannot be broken by the cares, stresses, and evils of this world and life itself. What natural home insurance policy can provide this coverage to you? The winds and storms will come, but when The Lord shelters you, you may feel the sting and the rain, but that is all you will feel. You are covered.

When you abide and dwell in the Secret Place of God, you will say:

<u>"Surely He shall deliver you from the snare of the fowler And from the perilous pestilence." (Verse 3)</u>

Fowlers or hunters use a snare to catch animals. A snare is a trap; it is well-hidden. An unsuspecting animal can easily get caught and be killed. When you say surely, you are stating a fact, a firm belief, without doubt, you have total trust and confidence in the outcome. You know when you dwell and abide in the secret place of the Almighty, you have a firm assurance that God will deliver you from Satan's devices, traps, and schemes. No plot of Satan's will succeed because the eyes of God are watching; the Holy Spirit is hovering over us as He resides in us. The fiery darts will come, but they will not penetrate. The noisome pestilence can't affect us.

Pestilence is a deadly disease that affects entire communities and nations. They will come, but when you are in His presence, it will not affect you. You may succumb to the disease, but the disease doesn't have the final authority over you. When you make your home the habitation of God's shadow, He shields you from destruction. He protects you from ordinary pestilence and perilous pestilences, such as pandemics and epidemics that cripple communities and nations.

It is not to say that the righteous won't be affected by pestilence. In pandemics and epidemics, the righteous have died, such as in the recent COVID 19 pandemic in 2020. There were righteous men and women who died as a result of getting COVID 19. There are righteous people who are stricken by diseases and have died as a result. Every person is appointed to death; when that appointment is, no one but God knows: *"And as it is appointed for men to die once, but after this the judgment,"* Hebrews 9:27. However, in the righteous case, they were protected by God. Also, God does protect us by giving us godly wisdom, guidance, and instruction on how to take care of our bodies, live healthy lifestyles, and protect the environment. If you abuse your body, the possibility of death may come sooner.

In the Divine Insurance Policy, in the secret place:

<u>"He shall cover you with His feathers, And under His wings you shall take refuge; His truth shall be your shield and buckler" (Verse 4)</u>

Metaphorically, God does not have wings. He is a Spirit: *"God is Spirit, and those who worship Him must worship in spirit and truth,"* John 4:24. Here, the psalmist refers to God's protection as a mother bird protecting her babies with her wings. In the case of an eagle, in the natural, the adult eagle is crouched above her babies with her body slightly opened, shielding and protecting them from the winds, heat, other weather, and prey. In the event of danger, the eagle spreads her large wings and brings her baby into her breast, and then she covers the baby underneath her body until you can't see the baby anymore. The only thing you will see is the mother eagle, sitting still watching her surroundings. The baby is safe from hurt, harm, or danger. In the storm or danger, the mother eagle is not distracted by the storm; she focuses only on protecting her baby. When we abide in the secret place of God, this is what God does for us. He covers us with His mighty power, and under His power (wings), He brings us closer to Him, and under Him, protecting us from the wiles of the enemy and the evils of the world. Like the baby eagle, we stay under our covering and protection as God keeps us. Under His covering, we are safe and our only focus is to remain in His protection and His covering. When we are in this place, storms may come, but we are fully assured that He, our God, is protects us from them.

His Truth shall be your shield and buckler: God's Truth is His word. When we are operating in the Truth, not only does it make us free (John 8:31), but it is also our buckler. We have the shield of faith that protects and covers us, but we also have His buckler. The buckler is a small round shield held by a handle at arm's length; it allows God's word to keep the fiery darts of the enemy at arm's length, providing more protection while we are under His wings. It's saying, NO Satan, you can't touch this one. He is under my protection. Like in a Marvel superhero movie, the buckler is thrust out, symbolizing that whatever is coming our way while we are under His wings has to stop. It cannot come any further. It depicts the traffic **"STOP"** sign. The Truth causes it to stop.

The Reflection of Jesus, The Christ in Us

Therefore because God is covering us:

"You shall not be afraid of the terror by night, Nor of the arrow that flies by day." (Verse 5)

God as a shelter and refuge gives us strength and courage. Many people are afraid of the unknown; they are fearful of the what if or what might happen: the bad doctor's report, a layoff, a major storm on the way, the terrors and evils in this world. When you dwell in the secret place of God, God is saying, I have you. The Blood covers you. The insurance policy is PAID IN FULL. The contract is valid; there are no hidden agenda or fine print. You don't have to be afraid of what is coming your way, or a bad report, a layoff, or a calamity. Isaiah 41:10 promises us that God has us. *"Fear thou not; for I am with thee: be not dismayed; for I am thy God: I will strengthen thee; yea, I will help thee; yea, I will uphold thee with the right hand of my righteousness."*

When Satan's arrows come, causing us to doubt and fear, God lifts up a standard, and that standard is Christ Jesus. *"So shall they fear the name of the LORD from the west, and his glory from the rising of the sun. When the enemy shall come in like a flood, the Spirit of the LORD shall lift up a standard against him,"* Isaiah 59:19. In that standard, *God has not given us a spirit of fear; He has given us power, love and a sound mind,"* 2 Timothy 1:7). So, we don't have to fear the arrows that fly by day because the LORD has us, and if God is for us, then our divine protection plan keeps anything against us. We don't have to be afraid of anything that comes our way.

We don't have to be afraid of:

"Nor of the pestilence that walks in darkness, Nor of the destruction that lays waste at noonday." (Verse 6)

The LORD keeps us from the assaults of the enemy and the destruction of the world. We can rest in knowing whatever season we are in, we are overcomers and conquerors in HIM (*"Yet in all these things we are more than conquerors through Him who loved us,"* Romans 8:37.) Sometimes the season may be a season of darkness, uncertainty, and pain, and we can't see the path in front of us. However, the Lord's word is always a lamp unto our feet, and it guides us as it shines that path for us to walk. The Psalmist says, *"Your word is a lamp to my feet, And a light to my path,"* Psalm 119:105. Even in the midst of the storm and darkness, the Light shines through. In the nighttime, when we put our total trust in Him, He gives sleep to His beloved: *"It is vain for you to rise up early, To sit up late, To eat the bread of sorrows; For so He gives His beloved sleep,"* Psalm 127:2.

In His Divine Insurance Plan:

"A thousand may fall at your side, And ten thousand at your right hand; But it shall not come near you." (Verse 7)

In His secret place, hidden room, no weapon can come against you. *"No weapon formed against you shall prosper, And every tongue which rises against you in judgment You shall condemn. This is the heritage of the servants of the LORD, And their righteousness is from Me,"* Says the LORD,*"* Isaiah 54:17. Whatever opposes you or comes against you cannot stand. You will see it fall because the Lord will fight your battle. Regardless of how many fall from plagues, sicknesses, pestilences, or other dangers, you shall continue to stand in the battle. Great security is promised to Believers during turbulence and dangerous times. God's mercy and His goodness and kindness keep us from falling into the enemy's snares and traps. The temptation will come, for every man is tempted, but when our trust is in Our God, when we are dwell in His Secret Place, He delivers us even from temptations. Others may fall into the temptation, but we don't because our trust is in our God. We are covered in His shelter. Therefore, no matter how many fall on the right side or left side of you, you will continue to stand.

And when the battle is over, and the smoke has cleared, and you can see, in God's divine insurance plan, the reward of the wicked:

<u>"Only with your eyes shall you look, And see the reward of the wicked." (Verse 8)</u>

When we look at the world, we wonder why the wicked and evil prosper and have massive wealth. Doesn't God see them? Whereas, when we stand for God and His righteousness, it seems our entire Christian walk or journey is a battle. It appears that we are constantly attacked, bruised, and worn down by the enemy and the world's system. There is a saying that the rich get richer, and the poor get poorer. Never before in the history of our country has there been a significant wealth gap such as this time. Food, gas, and housing prices have soared, and it appears that the only ones benefiting are those who say there is no God or do not believe in God. From this perspective, it is easy to get discouraged, doubtful, and full of envy. However, the Lord tells us not to envy the wicked, for surely their time will come. There are many scriptures that show us how God will deal with the wicked.

- Psalm 37:28, "For the Lord loves justice and does not

forsake His godly ones; They are preserved forever, But the descendants of the wicked will be cut off."

• Psalm 37:38, "But transgressors will be altogether destroyed; the posterity of the wicked will be cut off."

• 1 Peter 3:12, "For the eyes of the Lord are toward the righteous, And His ears attend to their prayer, But the face of the Lord is against those who do evil."

• Psalm 11:5, "The LORD tests the righteous, but his soul hates the wicked and the one who loves violence."

Psalm 37:1-2, 7-9 tells us not to envy the wicked: "*Do not fret because of evildoers, Nor be envious of the workers of iniquity. For they shall soon be cut down like the grass....*" "*Rest in the LORD AND wait patiently for Him; Do not fret because of him who prospers in his way, Because of the man who brings wicked schemes to pass. Cease from anger and forsake wrath; Do not fret—it only causes harm. For evildoers shall be cut off.*"

Our responsibility until Jesus comes back is to do good, trust God, delight ourselves in the Lord, and don't worry about the evildoers. God sees them. They are not fooling Him. Galatians 6:7 informs us that they will reap the harvest they have sown. "*Do not be deceived, God is not mocked; for whatever a man sows, that he will also reap. For he who sows to his flesh will of the flesh reap corruption, but he who sows to the Spirit will of the Spirit reap everlasting life.*" The unrighteousness will eventually get what is coming to them. It is in God's hands and timing, so we don't focus or concern ourselves with what they are doing. Our focus should be to continue to dwell in the secret place of the Most High.

When we do this, we are safe in His hands:

"Because you have made the Lord, who is my refuge, Even the Most High, your dwelling place." (Verse 9) "No evil shall befall you, Nor shall any plague come near your dwelling" (Verse 10) "For He shall give His angels charge over you, To keep you in all your ways." (Verse 11)

Angels are supernatural beings created by God as servants and instruments to do His will. They have specific roles: they issue proclamations, deliver warnings, interpret visions, conduct God's will on earth, and protect and care for believers until Jesus comes back. There are three types of angels, Cherubim, Seraphim, and living creatures. The two angels mentioned in the Bible are Gabriel, the messenger of God, and Michael, the protector or warrior.

When you are under the umbrella of God's protection, one of the ways He provides protections for you is through His angels commanding them to keep and bear you up. Angels are commissioned from the Lord to watch over God's children. They are called our guardians- hence guardian angels. Angels minister and provide comfort and strength to us, as they did with Jesus after He was tempted in the wilderness by the devil and in the Garden of Gethsemane.

"Then the devil left Him, and angels came and ministered to Him," Matthew 4:11.

"And He withdrew from them about a stone's throw, and He knelt down and began to pray, 42saying, "Father, if You are willing, remove this cup from Me; yet not My will, but Yours be done." 43Now an angel from heaven appeared to Him, strengthening Him," Luke 22:41-43.

Angels patrol the earth as God's representatives and will be with Jesus when He returns. They carry out God's will on earth and help Believers to overcome the snares of the enemy. God commands His angels to guard and protect us. *"The [angel of the LORD encamps all around those who fear Him, And delivers them,"* Psalm 34:7. Angels keep us in all from hurt, harm and danger, and even temptations. There is a saying that you never know who you are entertaining. It may be an angel.

They keep us from stumbling:

"In their hands they shall bear you up, Lest you dash your foot against a stone," (Verse 12)

Psalm 91:11 states that God will give His angels charge over us and keep us in all of our ways, here in verse 12, it states how they will perform their duties. The more we stay hidden in the secret place of God, the more power the angels have to keep us from hardships and struggles, and the less we are likely to suffer from the consequences of sin because angels are watching over us, protecting us. This doesn't mean that sometimes we won't slip or fall, but God's angels are right there beside us to minister to us and pick us up while comforting us. As with a mother with her young child, they gently guide us and put us back on track, nourishing us from our wounds and hurts until we are strong enough to stand again. As wounded soldiers, they carry us out of the battle to the Great Physician. They continue to be by our side as we are being operated on in the spiritual, caring for us, wiping away the tears, and healing and bandaging our wounds. They are with us at all times. They protect us from unseen things, such as accidents or major destruction, as well as the seen. They provide warnings of things to come, as they did in Lot's case. God was about to destroy Sodom because of its wicked ways, but

He sent two angels to warn and rescue Lot (Genesis 19). When we pray and speak God's Word, they respond to the Word. They carry us to safety and watch over us. Even in difficulties and obstacles, we are protected.

And as the angels of the LORD protect us, we then can tread upon the lion and the cobra:

"You shall tread upon the lion and the cobra, The young lion and the serpent you shall trample underfoot." (Verse 13)

Regardless of how strong or fierce the enemy is, the Believer under God's divine protection plan will rise to victory, and the enemy will succumb to defeat. The lion shall lie prostrate at the feet of the Believer, and the serpent, regardless of how poisonous the venom is, will not affect the Believer who dwells in the secret place of the Most High. The Apostle Paul is a great example. When bitten by a poisonous snake, he shook it off and continue on his mission. The poison didn't affect him (Acts 28:5). In 2 Chronicles 20: 15 & 17, God tells us what He is going to do to the enemy. He lets us know that this battle is not ours, but His; therefore, we can rest knowing the strong beast is a defeated foe. So, when you are facing what seems unsurmountable when you are dwelling in the His secret place, know that God has you:

"And he said, "Listen, all you of Judah and you inhabitants of Jerusalem, and you, King Jehoshaphat! Thus says the LORD to you: 'Do not be afraid nor dismayed because of this great multitude, for the battle is not yours, but God's." 2 Chronicles 20:15.

"You will not need to fight in this battle. Stand firm, hold your position, and see the salvation of the LORD on your behalf, O

Judah and Jerusalem.' Do not be afraid and do not be dismayed. Tomorrow go out against them, and the LORD will be with you," 2 Chronicles 20:17.

If you combine all the forces in the world, including Satan's evil devices, NOTHING can overcome God's ability to protect us from danger. God's power is Dunamis.

The God, the Insurer's Promises (Verses 14-16)

In the first part of Psalm 91, verses 1-13, the Psalmist provides the stipulation to receive full coverage or access to God's divine insurance plan. To dwell or abode in His secret place gets you full coverage and protection. The Believer will receive certain benefits when you follow the guidelines and instructions of God's word. The last three verses, 14-16 of Psalm 91, is the Insurer, God Himself telling you what He will do for those who dwell permanently in His secret place. You have some responsibilities to do, but when you meet the obligations, God is saying to you: *Because you set your love upon me, I will deliver you. When you call on me, I will answer you, and finally, I will give you long life and show you My salvation.* God speaks promises and blessings over His people, specifically to those who set their love upon Him. In the last three passages of the psalm, God is confirming and expanding His promises. God demonstrates what He will do to those who live in His presence:

"Because he has set his love upon Me, therefore I will deliver him; I will set him on high, because he has known My name."
(Verse 14)

The LORD is saying here, because you choose to dwell and abide in my secret place, to live in me, I will provide you not just refuge, deliverance, and protection, but because you have the premium policy, I am going to set you on high. All the world will see that you belong to me. My light will shine through you. The Bible says we are the light of the world.

When we first receive salvation, there is joy. There is a love and hunger for God and His word. We thirst after Him. However, soon as the thirst is watered and the hunger is fed, our zeal leaves, we become Christians with dim lights. However, those who continue to have zeal, hunger, and thirst after God and His word, and put their trust in God; who seek and hunger after Him; who dwell in His Secret Place are the ones God is speaking to in these verses. This is the Believer who will see the fullness of God's Dunamis power. This is the man God delights in, who God finds pleasure in. The Believer who God promises to deliver and protect because this Believer clings to Him in love. He delights himself in the Lord. He longs to be with the Lord. Intimacy with the Lord is his main objective; getting to know Jesus while allowing the Holy Spirit to infuse his entire being is his quest.

Because this person enjoys spending time with the Lord, listening to the Lord, allowing God's Holy Spirit to guide and lead him, reading the Word, getting to know more of God, trusting God with all his heart and not leaning on his own understanding, (Proverbs 3:5), God is pleased with him. When you are in this state of trusting, the divine insurance policy takes full effect because you acknowledge God as your Savior, your Source, and your total confidence in Him. You have submitted your will to His will and plans for you (Jeremiah 29:11). When you function like this, God is saying here based on His Word and promises, He is going to show you off. He is going to exhort you so others will see you and know that HE IS your God. Because you choose to endure the hardships, trials, persecution, pain and weeping, He will bring you joy ("*weeping may endure for a night, but joy comes in the morning*," Psalm 30:5). You stayed under His covering; you were willing to go through because you love Him and put your complete reliance and hope in Him. Because you lived by faith in Him (the just shall live by faith), He is going to bless you. This is what the insurance policy curtails...the full benefits when you have followed the guidelines and stipulations. When the storm comes, and you didn't waiver; you still trusted in the Lord, then you can reap the full benefits and more.

When we set our love upon God, He says:

<u>"He shall call upon Me, and I will answer him; I will be with him in trouble; I will deliver him and honor him."</u> (Verse 15)

When we have found favor in God's sight, we can ask, and the word says He will answer us and deliver us. This is where the Army of the Lord, the Lord of Host, comes in. His Dunamis power keeps us from all hurt and trouble. No weapon formed against us will prosper, and every tongue that rises against us will not stand. He will fight our battles and contend with those who contend with us. God is saying, If I am for you, nothing and no one can be against you. I have you because I see my Son's reflection in you. I see Me, my Righteousness in you. I smell the sweet aroma of your worship and obedience. I see your surrendering of your will. The storms will come, the flooding will come, but you are covered by the Most High.

When you pray to me, I will answer you. The fervent prayers of the righteous...call upon me and I will show you...When you call upon Me, I will show you great and mighty things. Here we have full access to God's promises. We have the assurance that

He will deliver us, and because we honor God, He will honor us. God promises to answer the prayer of the one who loves Him; who genuinely knows Him as God. He promises to be and answer that person in times of trouble, rescuing him from the trouble. *"Many are the afflictions of the righteous, But the LORD delivers him out of them all,"* Psalm 34:19.

And finally,

"With long life I will satisfy him And show him My salvation." (Verse 16)

We have eternal life with God. However, here God is saying, while you are on the earth, portraying my reflection on the earth, your life will be long and satisfying. Jesus said in John 10: 10, "The thief comes to steal, kill and deceive, but I came to give life and more abundantly." Jesus was talking about the "ZOE" kind of life. The Lord promises long and satisfying life to those who trust and love Him.

God is saying under His divine insurance plan that He will show us His salvation. He will show us His power, His Goodness, and His wisdom. In this place of intimacy with God, you will see the infinite depths and heights of the spiritual realm, allowing you to see other facets of the Glory of the Almighty God, as John did in the Book of Revelation. Things seen and unseen, the breadth of His salvation in eternity to come, the completion and fullness of salvation for eternity to come.

The purpose of Psalm 91 is to portray the Hesed (love: mercy, kind, gracious---all compelling) the Father has for us. *"For God so loved the world (us), He gave His only begotten son,"* John 3:16. Psalm 91 reflects His love. In this psalm, the Believers have total coverage for living successful and productive lives while on earth. Everything is covered: protection, security, and most of all, the promises of God to deliver, keep and protect us from dangers seen and unseen. When we put our total trust and confidence in God, He, in return, protects us and keeps us. As Jesus prayed, *"Father keep them from the evil one"* John 17:15. No man-made insurance policy can provide this type of coverage or protection.

As Believers, we have access to the greatest policy ever written; it provides everything we need to live on this earth successfully, productively, and for Him. We know we are fully covered when danger comes when we grasp what we have in God and His promises. We don't have to worry because the policy is **PAID IN FULL!** We only have to meet one criterion.

When we know who God is, we can dwell in His presence and live in His secret place; it is, after all, the safest place for the Believer.

PART III

The Womb of God Upon the Earth Throuh Prayer

The Womb of God Upon the Earth Throuh Prayer

In the natural, when we hear the word womb, our mind immediately thinks of a place in a woman's body where an unborn baby is developed. From a single cell to molecules and atoms inside the womb, a life is growing, creating an unknown to a known, an inorganic to an organic, and eventually, a fully developed baby in nine months. For the unborn child, inside the womb is a place of security and safety. The unborn child doesn't have to go outside of the womb, its cocoon. Everything it needs is provided until it is developed and has all the essentials to live outside its corridors. Only then is it forced out of the birth canal into the complexity of its new world. Before then, the unborn child lives in an environment provided by the one carrying it. It's in a resting stage, a dormant and peaceful place, where there is no pressure and no commitment. In this place of security and comfort, it only has to eat, sleep, and grow. There are no worries or cares. Its only responsibility is to function according to the nature of the environment in the world it knows.

Although the unborn child is in a restful place, there is activity taking place. It's growing and developing as it rests. The unborn child develops hands, feet, and vital organs. The gender is identified. Also, its genetic makeup by both parent's DNA is established. During the stages of the pregnancy, the sonogram depicts its continuing development and growth, bringing tears of joy to the parents and other supporting members. During the many weeks in the womb, the unborn child continues to grow.

The nose, ears, and eyes are formed, and it begins to grow in inches. There is some movement, such as touching its nose and mouth, but for the most part, while in the dwelling place of the womb, its total dependency is on the keeper of the womb, it's mother.

As the unborn child continues to develop and grow inside the womb, another aspect of the birthing process is taking place: the preparation for the coming of the child. The mother is preparing for its birth. She attends the birthing classes; she reads all the necessary books and googles everything to prepare for the big day. Her husband or a designated person to be with her helps her prepare for the birth day. She has a baby shower and receives many gifts to help with the caring of the baby. The baby's room is decorated according to the gender of the child. Everything is in place for the main event. After months of waiting, the time has come, the baby's due date finally arrives. The woman is both thrilled and overwhelmed. However, in the final stages of the birthing process, it is only then, she realizes that no one or nothing, family, physician, friends, books, or movies, could prepare her for the beautiful yet piercing journey of childbirth.

As the mother prepares for the birth in the outer court, the unborn child's due date arrives. When the child is ready to come forth, there is an unusual amount of activity in the womb. The body is preparing for the unborn child to be released. When the pressures of the unborn child have grown to its full capacity and no longer can the womb secure and accommodate a place for its occupant, causing disruption and disorder in the womb, it is time for the birthing of the child. Soon the unborn child's world will no longer exist. To move into its next world, the surrounding pressures of life in the womb become chaotic; the unborn child can no longer live in the womb; it has to be pushed out to fully grow and manifest into what it needs to be and do in its next world.

When the womb carrying the unborn child is ready to push, it opens up the passage, or the birth canal, and gives access for the fully grown child to go through. The passage is small in compared to the child; however, as the child goes through, it expands as needed and will continue to do so, causing great pressure and pain to the mother. The womb doesn't focus on the mother's discomfort and pain, its only mission is to keep the unborn child until it is ready to be released and then releases it when it is time. The womb is designed for this function. To keep the baby in the womb would be detrimental for both the baby and the mother, causing one or both to be deeply wounded or even die in the process. If the baby dies in the womb, the life it was to be will never be manifested.

During the birthing process, there is travailing, groaning, wailing, and crying out from the mother as the physicians and her loved one tells her to push and continue to push. She cries out in pain that she can't, but the more she cries out, she continues to push through the pain. The breakage or tears of the perineal because the baby's head is too large for the opening causes the woman extreme agony and pain. The tears help the baby break through the portal. The sharp pain is extremely intense and excruciating as the baby's head breaks through the wall and tears the outer canal. The woman falls back and gives up her strength, only to rely on the power within her. Following her body's instructions, she succumbs to the birth process. She realizes her body was created to bring forth birth. It's no longer her strength or might but the power within her body's functions. Like the womb, her body knows what to do, so it doesn't take its cues from the woman, but from the One who created it to function. During the birthing process, the climax of the baby coming can be compared to a near death experience. However, when the baby's head appears, followed by the rest of the body, the moment of relief comes, and then joy, as the woman sees the baby, her child for the first time. Although there is some numbness, the pain is not as intense. When she sees her precious child, and takes it in her arms, with tears of joy, she knows everything she had to go through was worth the process. The travailing, the pain, the crying out, and even the tearing of her body was worth the reward of her new baby.

We can view the natural birthing process or journey in the same way as the spiritual birthing of our prayers manifested in the earth. Each prayer has a process to go through, and each has established instructions and functions to follow. As Believers, as with an unborn child in its mother's womb, we are children of God, and the womb that we are living in until Jesus comes back for us is the earth. The earth is the Lord and the fullness thereof, "*The earth is the LORD's, and all its fullness, The world and those who dwell therein,*" Psalm 24:1. Everything we need, the Lord has provided for us. Our life was created by Him and for Him; therefore, what we need is in Him. As the unborn baby in the mother's womb depends on everything from the mother, the nutrients, the blood, oxygen, and its lifeline, our total dependency and trust of answered prayers come from our God. However, just as the natural birthing process brings pain, our answered prayers are also a process or journey of pain. The pain is not necessarily physical, but a spiritual, a breaking.

In the natural, the woman has a womb to carry the unborn child into full development. In the spiritual, we are the Womb of God upon the earth. We are regenerated through the Holy

Spirit and made through the likeness and character of Christ. Unlike the woman, whose body regenerates life, we do not generate life, but through our prayers, life is manifested. We release that life through the tenacity of prayer, then in Jesus, the tenacity of prayer begins to surface. When the prayer is about to be released into the atmosphere, just like a baby coming and the woman cries out in pain, there is pain and travailing when our prayers are coming. The Holy Spirit, along with the angels, are there to assist us in pushing, as they hold us up in His strength and power. We pray until something happens (**PUSH**) in Him, travailing while emerging into a spiritual phenomenon through the Holy Spirit, such as groaning, weeping, and crying out physically while continuing pressing and pushing. As we begin to develop in this place, our nutrients and lifeline comes from the Word of God and the Blood of Jesus. As we continue to pray His word, we begin to form in His likeness and character.

During this time of intense prayer, there is a spiritual war raging, as in the natural birth, it feels as if you are close to death. Why? Our prayers are battles grounds as we wait for God to move. The scripture says, *"And from the days of John the Baptist until now the kingdom of heaven suffers violence, and the violent take it by force,"* Matthew 11:12. Every time there is a prayer going up to heaven, the enemy is determined by any means necessary to stop our prayer. Therefore, our prayers should never be passive but active and fully confident in knowing that God hears us and wants to answer us. However, we must come to Him in the petition and the position of who He is (*"Let us therefore come boldly to the throne of grace, that we may obtain mercy and find grace to help in time of need,"* Hebrews 4:16). John 10:10 says the thief comes only to steal, kill and destroy; it is the same way with our prayers. Satan's job is to deter or disrupt our prayers by keeping us disconnected from God. Our position is to go through the process in full force, believing and knowing that God has already provided the answer. As we cry out to Him, our position is to pray without ceasing as we wait for His answer. Just like the body knows its function as it relates to giving birth, we are created to function according to our makeup, the image of God.

The good news is that we are not alone in our travailing and wailing as we wait for the manifestation of the power of God's answer. The Holy Spirit, our Paraclete, a type of midwife in the process, is our Comforter. He is at our side to assist us with the birthing pains of prayer. (The Greek word translated "Comforter" or "Counselor" is parakletos…." one called to the side to another). Under the unction of the Holy Spirit, we are guided to continue to push until the prayer is birthed. It is in this setting or atmosphere, the right time, for such a moment, heaven touches earth, and the answered prayer is released in the Kairos atmosphere. It comes at the appointed time, or as we say, in the right place, at the right time. When our prayers are answered, it is a Kairos moment in time.

The word Kairos means a propitious moment for decision or action. The word kairos (prounouced KAI-ros)was an ancient Greek word meaning "opportunity," "season," or "fitting time. Kairos represents a kind of 'qualitative' time, as in 'the right time'. It means taking advantage of or even creating a perfect moment to deliver a particular message. "In Ancient Greek, the word kairos (pronounced 'KAI-ros') means 'time' – but not just any time. It's about timeliness: the special moment when it's the opportune time to say or do a particular thing."[5]

The Bible uses the word kairos and its cognates 86 times

5   https://boords.com/ethos-pathos-logos/what-is-kairos

in the New Testament (e.g., in Matthew 8:29; Luke 19:44; and Acts 24:25). The word often includes the idea of an opportunity or a suitable time for an action to take place. When we "seize the day," we are taking advantage of the kairos given to us. A kairos is a time when things "come to a head," requiring decisive action. There was "an appointed time" for John the Baptist to be born (Luke 1:20). It was a kairos time when Jesus was born. Each of these uses of kairos denotes a unique time in which something special was to happen.[6] Kairos is a time when conditions are right for the accomplishment of a crucial action. Jesus came at the right Kairos of time; the civil rights movement in the sixties was a Kairos moment in time, and what's happening today in the world as it relates to race relations in America is a Kairos moment in time.

Another word for time is "Chronos." Chronos represents time as we know, such as what time is it? Do you see the time? The time is 8 o'clock. Chronos emphasizes the duration of the time, an appointed time, whereas, as Kairos, there is no regard for the length of the time; it's timeless. Unfortunately for many, we don't operate in the Chronos of time. When it comes to prayer, many of us live in the Chronos of time. Our day-to-day activities, our daily jobs or routines, our recreational activities, even in ministry, our work for God, we operate in the Chonos. Rarely do we operate in the Kairos time, praying for God's will to be birthed on earth and waiting for it to be manifested, and in our wait, dwelling in God's secret place, while continuing to pray until the prayer is birthed into the atmosphere.

When we operate on God's timing, as the unborn child develops in the womb, we too are developing in the womb of the secret place, hidden in God. In the womb, there are unlimited

6   https://www.gotquestions.org/kairos-meaning.html

possibilities, full potentials; it is fertile and abundant. It's the place of beginning, a place of rest and development, creativity, and purpose. When we operate in that place, inviting the Holy Spirit in our prayer, the Chronos becomes Kairos. His DNA transforms us into His likeness, and we begin to take on His attributes and characteristics, as Genesis 1:26 states, *"Then God said, "Let Us make man in Our image, according to Our likeness; let them have dominion over the fish of the sea, over the birds of the air, and over the cattle, over all the earth and over every creeping thing that creeps on the earth." So God created man in His own image; in the image of God He created him; male and female He created them."*

When we become more like God, we open our ears and heart to anticipate and recognize the Kairos of the Holy Spirit, sensing His presence, guiding and showing us what to pray according to the will of the Father. And when we do this, the scripture, Romans 8:26-27, becomes a reality: *"Likewise the Spirit also helps in our weaknesses. For we do not know what we should pray for as we ought, but the Spirit Himself makes intercession for us with groanings which cannot be uttered. Now He who searches the hearts knows what the mind of the Spirit is, because He makes intercession for the saints according to the will of God."* We become impregnated with God's Holy Word, and the profoundness of our prayers becomes meaningful and purpose-driven for God's will on the earth. We pray according to His will and plans.

When this takes place, there is a moment of rest…**SELAH**; and we become the womb, and the baby becomes our prayers on the earth. As the pregnant woman carries the unborn child, preparing her body and mind for the birthing process, with our praying hands, God through the seeding and the cultivating of our baby (our prayers), empowers us with the desire of the intimacy of prayer. Under the unction of the Holy Spirit, God dresses us in His attire as we SELAH. The word SELAH in Greek means both to pause or ponder and praise; you are pondering over God's word as you draw closer to Him; whereas, at the same time, you are in a place of praise because you are coming into the full understanding of who God is. In this moment of Kairos, God is perfecting us and preparing us for the prayer to be released. Then at that moment, close to the birthing, you begin travailing, moaning, groaning, and crying, releasing a spiritual phenomenon in the atmosphere. This is when you start to feel the pain. The labor and the unction to pray sincereness in Him. You get an unction, a drive to pray.

When a woman is in labor, she begins to feel the pain, and as she cries out, she begins to push through the pain. When the woman approaches the climax part of the delivery, she begins to sigh a breath of relief. The baby is here, or in our case, the prayer is answered. When the prayer is released, you get an urgency to pray for somebody on their death bed or in trouble. In the natural, the woman goes through the hollering, the pain, but in the spiritual aspect, when you began to reach that climax, God gives you that unction to feel the spiritual pain that He is about to release the prayer. It's coming, it hurts, the baby is coming, but in the spiritual, you feel the sharp pain, the tearing, and you're at the breaking point. It is in this traumatic state the Holy Spirit comforts you.

In those Kairos moments, the guiding of the Holy Spirit will give us the unction to pray for our loved ones or specific seasons and events in time. You can be driving, and all of a sudden, you have an urgency to pray for someone or something; it's in your spiritual belly. You have to pray right at that moment. There's an urgency to pray, and people may wonder what is wrong with you. You can't explain it, but you know God is calling you to pray **RIGHT THEN**. In the Hebrew term Kairos, the Holy Spirit is letting you feel the danger or urgency. He's letting you know it's dangerous for someone, so you immediately stop and pray for them. It's almost similar to the woman getting ready to experience the labor pain because the baby is getting ready to come. She gets severe pain. In us, it's the Holy Spirit letting us know the enemy is about to attack someone (Luke 4:13 and Luke 8:13) or someone is in extreme danger. That's why the word tells us to be alert at all times: *"Be sober, be [vigilant; because your adversary the devil walks about like a roaring lion, seeking whom he may devour,"* 1 Peter 5:8.

Like the baby in the natural is connected to the mother, and the blood transpires, giving the baby the nutrients it needs to thrive and survive while developing. As we connect to God through prayer, praying to Him, His Word, and His will, the praying hands in the womb on the Bible, God gives us the nutrients to survive and thrive. We have the whole armor of God on, and we are operating in the fullness of Jesus Christ. We begin to feel the life of the Holy Spirit manifesting and empowering us, as we can cry out, "Our Father," "My Intimacy," "My Daddy," recognizing who He is.

When you are in this spiritual prostate position; proving yourself; you can say Our Father (ABBA Father), as stated in Romans 8:14, *"For as many as are led by the Spirit of God, these are sons of God."* He promotes you as you cry out to Him because you're in a position of intimacy with Him. He is your Daddy and your Father. He released you from the pain and agony of birthing the prayer. Now you are the joint-heirs with Christ. He gives you that intimate Dunamis power.

Unfortunately for many Believers, we don't experience God in this manifestation. We have seminars, programs, schools,, and training on praying or how to pray; however, for many, there is no great power or total breakthrough in our prayers. Sadly, many Believers' prayer life isn't as effective as God wants. In the womb of God, our hands are in the praying mold. We are praying for God's will and for the enemy to be defeated. We are prostrate before Him, quietly waiting, but this is far and few between the triumphs, breakthroughs and supernatural. God is not concerned with our lofty words or our long prayers. He wants to bring His fire on the earth, and our prayers are the vessels or tools to make it happen.

Jesus said in Matthew 6: 5-8, *"And when you pray, you shall not be like the hypocrites. For they love to pray standing in the synagogues and on the corners of the streets, that they may be seen by men. Assuredly, I say to you, they have their reward. But you, when you pray, go into your room, and when you have shut your door, pray to your Father who is in the secret place; and your Father who sees in secret will reward you openly. And when you pray, do not use vain repetitions as the heathen do. For they think that they will be heard for their many words."* Jesus was very specific about prayer. He told the disciples to not be like hypocrites, wasting time with meaningless words, being pretentious.

Jesus' disciples saw how John taught his disciples. They wanted to know how to pray effectively. They asked Jesus to teach them how to pray. "Now it came to pass, as He was praying in a certain place, when He ceased, that one of His disciples said to Him, "Lord, teach us to pray, as John also taught his disciples." He said to them, "When you pray, say:

"Our Father in heaven, Hallowed be Your name. Your kingdom come. Your will be done On earth as it is in heaven. Give us this day our daily bread. And forgive us our debts, As we forgive our debtors. And do not lead us into temptation, But deliver us from the evil one. For Yours is the kingdom and the power and the glory forever," Matthew 6:9-13 and Luke 11:1-4.

The Lord's Prayer, or the disciples' prayer, is a profound way to connect to the Holy God. Jesus wanted His disciples including us, His Bride, to pray always acknowledging first, who God is: His nature, characteristics, and attributes. Secondly, pray according to His will and purpose on the earth until Jesus comes back for us. Thirdly, recognize His position, and come to Him in adoration, praise, and honor. Remember, we are reflecting Him and not us.

Jesus said to pray:

Acknowledgment: <u>Our Father in Heaven, Hallowed Be Your Name:</u>

We must come knowing that God is God, and He is greatly to be revered and honored; set apart; to keep holy. We pray according to His names and attributes: His names: Elohim. You have to seek the LORD, Creator of heaven and earth and dwell (live) in His presence, El Shadday. Most High – in Hebrew, it is Elyon. It means lofty, elevation, and supreme. Most High denotes God's supreme authority over all other authorities. Almighty – in Hebrew, it is Shadday. It means most powerful, denoting that in the vast universe, there is no power greater than God Discovering as a mere man His fullness- His attributes-His eternity, all-knowing, all present, and all-seeing God—His Holiness, His righteousness.

"The name of God is God, Himself." (John Wesley).

God resides in Heaven, not on earth. Pray according to where He lives. Heaven is not like the earth, so don't pray in the realm of the earth; pray in the spiritual realm. As you draw closer to God, He will draw closure to you (James 4:8), and as a result, you will be sitting with Jesus in heavenly places (Ephesians 2:6), knowing how His Kingdom operates.

Pray: <u>Your Kingdom Come:</u>

God's Kingdom came on the earth when Jesus came, died, and rose again. He left us the kingdom on earth, so we have to pray according to His will and way, not our wants or desires. God's desires and plans for the earth are to make His power rule and reign on earth, defeating the enemy, and freeing the captives, and healing the sick. God wants us to pray for His Kingdom to come on earth as it operates in heaven. He wants us to have abundant life on earth as Jesus said in John 10:10, *"...I came to give you life and life more abundantly."* That life is the "Zoe" kind of life of health to your whole being: body, mind, emotions, and relationships. Thy will is not passive; it's active. Therefore, when we come before the Lord, we don't come in fear and trembling, but in confidence in knowing that He is God and His Kingdom is already established on earth. We have to pray His Kingdom in, and sometimes we have to pray it in through travailing, groaning, weeping, and pain. Pray for God through the Holy Spirit to give you the power to create and release God's Dunamis power on earth.

Ask: <u>Your Will Be Done On Earth as it in Heaven:</u>

When Jesus went to the synagogue in Luke 4, He informed

the people and the leaders at that time what He was sent to earth to do:

"The Spirit of the LORD is upon Me, Because He has anointed Me To preach the gospel to the poor; He has sent Me to heal the brokenhearted, To proclaim liberty to the captives And recovery of sight to the blind, To set at liberty those who are oppressed; To proclaim the acceptable year of the LORD," Luke 4:16-19.

Jesus came to do the will of the Father. He came to preach the Gospel, the "Good News," to save the lost and restore us to our original state, back with the Father. He came to heal the brokenhearted, to set the captives free, make the blind see, free the oppressed, and establish the Kingdom of God on the earth. This is the Father's will. Anything else is not His will. We have to pray God's will, not man's. God is not interested in politics, political parties, or what's happening in our country or the world. He wants His will done on earth. Our responsibility as Believers is to submit to His will and pray for it to enter the earth.

Petition: <u>Give Us This Day Our Daily Bread:</u>

When the Israelites were wandering in the wilderness for forty years, they relied on God to provide them with manna each day, suffice for the day only and not another (Exodus 16). When a baby is in its mother's womb, it relies on the mother to provide for all its needs. We are to pray (ask) to God to give us what we need for the day. Jesus said, don't worry about tomorrow: *"Therefore do not worry about tomorrow, for tomorrow will worry about its own things. Sufficient for the day is its own trouble,"* Matthew 6:34. God is able and wants to provide for all of our needs. The Holy Spirit and His angels are here on earth to help us and provide us our needs. When we pray to God for His daily provisions, in return, He gives us His power and provisions to suffice us for the day. Whatever we need for the day to be more than conquerors or resist the enemy, causing him to flee, God can provide. Whatever He has called us to do, He can provide the provisions to accomplish the task. We have to pray according to what he desires and depend on Him for everything.

Ask: <u>And Forgive Us Our Debts as We Forgive Our Debtors:</u>

One of the Fruit of the Spirit is longsuffering. God is longsuffering. He delights in us with His patience. Like a loving Father, He gently waits for us with His goodness and mercy. Because God loves us, He forgave us, so we must also forgive others. In Luke 23:34, when Jesus was on the cross, He asked the Father to forgive them because they didn't know what they were doing: *"Then Jesus, said, "Father, forgive them for they do not know what they do."* Although this is a true statement for many, forgiveness is a stumbling block.

The past hurts and pain from loved ones always put us in the remembrance of what was done to us, the cruelty and shame, causing us to ponder, why should we forgive those who cause us so much pain and hurt. In the natural, when a mother is giving birth, the pain during childbirth is excruciating. In those nine months, she can become angry or upset during the process, the tearing of her body, the abnormalities, and unwelcome changes in her body. The unborn child is causing her so much pain and discomfort. We know we can't compare childbirth pain to molestation, rape, or other kinds of traumatic pain. However, your pain came into existence, Jesus wants you to forgive the person who caused the pain. Forgiving others is for you. When you forgive the person who caused you much grief, it sets you free.

God is God of vengeance; when you belong to Him, He will fight your battle. He wants you to forgive so you can have the life He created for you on earth.

When we forgive others, we receive God's mercies. God's mercies are new every morning. When we dwell in His secret place, we become more like Him, and the former way of our life slowly dissipates. Forgiveness requires deep travailing and wailing because that's when the baby's head is protruding out of the canal. It's the most pain because it's the breaking of the skin. When you forgive a person, there is a breaking; you are being torn from a soulish realm into a spiritual realm. The Good News is, the Holy Spirit is right there pushing you, as the angels act as the midwife, consoling you as you push.

Look at it from this perspective: Jesus forgave you. He took your scars, your pains, your lying spirit, murderous heart, adulterated ways, and yet, He loved you enough to say, "Father, forgive them for they don't know what they are doing or did. At that moment, He forgave us, and now, we will be with Him and the Father in glory for eternity.

Ask/Petition: <u>And Do Not Lead Us Into Temptation But Deliver Us From the Evil One:</u>

We know that God does not tempt us to sin (James 1:13). In our fallen state, we are sinners. Therefore, for us to be right again, Jesus came, died, and rose so we can be in right standing with God. There are times, like Jesus, we will go through or enter a wilderness experience (Matthew 4: 1-11), but that is to test our faith and make us stronger and more dependent on God. God desires us to be holy, for He is Holy. He knows that in our strength we cannot be holy. We need the Holy Spirit to teach us the ways of the Lord. Without the Lord's guidance, direction, and strength, the chance of the Believer entering into sin is great. Jesus said for us to pray to God to lead us not into temptation.

When we pray this, we are saying to God, "Lord, we want to be kept by You." When we are in His secret place, God keeps us, and the evil one cannot touch us because we have on God's full armor. Jesus tells us to flee. He said to resist the enemy, and when we resist him, he will flee. ("*Submit yourselves then, to Go. Resist the devil and he will flee from you,*"James 4:7d.) Our prayer is for God to lead us in His ways, keeping us from temptation, keeping anything or anyone away from us that causes temptation. When we face trials and tests, we rely on God's strength to keep us. We know that God is faithful, and He will keep us:

"God is faithful, who will not allow you to be tempted beyond what you are able, but with the temptation will also make the way of escape, that you may be able to bear it," I Corinthians 10:13.

We call on God when we are tempted.

Adoration and Praise: <u>For Yours is the Kingdom and the Power and the Glory Forever. Amen</u>

The prayer ends how it began with recognizing who God is with our adoration, praise, and honor to Him. We realize that our wisdom is foolish to God, and His thoughts are higher than ours. As we come to this understanding, we release our prayers to God to release them into the atmosphere as He sees fit.

Our greatest example of how to pray according to God's will is Jesus. Jesus taught His disciples to pray, but He also demonstrated to them the effectiveness of prayer according to what He taught. When we pray according to Jesus' instruction (the disciples/Lord's prayer), God's will, the Holy Spirit possesses our spirit, and holiness is saturated throughout our being, resulting in God's reflection manifesting on the earth.

We come to know God as ABBA Father, our Daddy; the intimacy of our relationships encircles our total being and trust in Him. We feel His tenderness and love. We become free, resulting in boldly coming to His throne in faith, petitioning Him with our needs, wants, and desires because we have merged into oneness with Him. Our wills, desires, and needs are according to His will for our lives. And so, we are praying what He put in us to pray. He creates in us the will to do what pleases Him. And as a result, we are lovers of His presence. We become transparent in Him for others to see His glory in our lives, reflecting on the spiritual process as we are being converted, becoming more like Jesus. We take on the character and likeness of Him.

The sum of it is:

~Make doing it our priority.
~Seek it as Christ did.
~Understand it and give it.
~Do it from the heart.
~For all to be saved.
~Not to be conformed to the world.
~To ask for His will.

This is the priestly prayer, the Celestial glory Jesus had from the beginning. Jesus told God to prepare Him a body. Before Jesus came to the earth, He ruled and reigned with God in heavenly places. (*"In the beginning was the Word, and the Word was with God, and the Word was God. He was in the beginning with God,"*

John 1:1-2.). For a Kairos moment, Jesus stepped out of His glory and stepped into humanity: John 17:5, *"And now, O Father, glorify Me together with Yourself, with the glory which I had with You before the world was."* The veil was not torn yet. However, going to the cross, Jesus understood who He was and where He came from; His home is in heavenly places. Jesus did not wait until He finished His assignment to glorify God, the Father. His entire life while on earth, through His faith and obedience, He glorified the Father.

Jesus dwelled in the secret place of God, and on earth, He prayed only according to the Father's will. During His earthly life, He, Jesus, was a man, and the Celestial glory that Jesus had from the beginning was temporarily hidden behind the veil. His assignment on earth was to teach the disciples and prepare the people for the Kingdom of God. He taught them God's way of doing things. When He died and rose, the veil was torn from the top to the bottom, bringing in the celestial glory of God to permeate the earth. There was no residue, only the fullness of Jesus the Christ, including His Dunamis power!

Jesus came to do the will of the Father. While on earth, He only demonstrated and performed the Father's will to the disciples and others. When Jesus rose and went back to the Father, He left His power for the Believers on the earth. He told the disciples to emulate what He taught them for the last three years. Their assignment was to preach and teach what Jesus taught them to the Body of Christ, spreading the Gospel of Jesus throughout the world until He came back for His Bride. When Jesus left, He promised them a Comforter, the Holy Spirit. The Holy Spirit was the force for them to complete their assignment. In the Holy Spirit, they went throughout the lands, preaching and teaching Jesus, and many people believed and received salvation.

The Reflection of Jesus, The Christ in Us

Today, over two thousand years later, Jesus' message to His Believers, the Body of Christ, is the same, to teach and spread the Gospel of Jesus Christ throughout the land. God's Dunamis power still resides in the earth. We have the ability within us to be like Jesus and spread His message throughout the world, doing the Father's will. We have the Holy Spirit to do it through us. We can't in our strength, but in His strength, we can. Through the power of God's Holy Spirit, we have the power to reflect God's image upon the earth.

"This is the word of the LORD to Zerubbabel: 'Not by might nor by power, but by My Spirit,' Says the LORD of hosts,"
Zachariah 4:6.

We have the power to move mountains, cast out demons, heal the sick, mend the brokenhearted, free the captives and oppressed, but most significantly, to infuse Jesus' reflection in the earth. That power comes from travailing, wailing, and crying out to God through our prayers in the womb, allowing God's Kairos time to be manifested on the earth. However, like the unborn child, it cannot manifest until there is a PUSH and prayers are prayed according to God's will. When this happens, our lives are changed from the impossible to the possible.

It's time for us to go into the birthing room and deliver our baby through prayer.

Conclusion

The natural man or un-regenerated man cannot know the things of God, even when it is right in his face. He lives in the natural state, a state that doesn't reflect God. When a person is *un-re*generated, he is not renewed in his heart or mind. He is not reborn in his spirit; his heart is unrepentant. He refuses to believe in the existence of God. Therefore, he cannot appreciate and see spiritual truths. The Word says this about the natural man, *"But the natural man does not receive the things of the Spirit of God, for they are foolishness to him; nor can he know them, because they are spiritually discerned,"* 1 Corinthians 2: 14.

While Jesus was earth, He taught in parables. Parables are not fairy tale stories or fables. They are illustrations that teach, guide, and direct the Believer to understand how God and His Kingdom operate. Parables are natural principles that we know that provide spiritual truth or revelations that we did not know. They are earthly stories depicting heavenly truths; intended to open the Believers' eyes to more profound revelations and insights, giving them greater understanding and perception of the spiritual realm. The natural man's wisdom keeps him from understanding Jesus' teachings. Jesus taught using parables to keep the natural man from understanding. Jesus told the disciples that He taught parables to conceal the truth from the foolish man: Matthew 13: 10-17.

Today, God still uses parables and illustrations; however, if one cannot see the obvious, it is dismissed as functioning in life as we know it or our daily existence. All around us, God's word is active; it's moving, bringing forth power, illumination, and advances to His Kingdom. The air we breathe, the food we grow on the land, the clothes we wear, and the homes we purchase or build all come from God. If we look closely, we can see how the Kingdom of God operates in all of these.

Unfortunately, in man's wisdom and foolishness, he took the spiritual things of God and made them into his everyday existence of life. The wedding ceremony, buying insurance, and the unborn child's birth all have a deeper revelation of how God operates in the spiritual realm. You have to be in a position of spiritual submission to see what God reveals in the open, in the natural.

The Bride of Christ is the marriage between the Church (Believers) and Christ. A better way to understand the Bride of Christ preparing for her wedding day is to illustrate this by using it in a parable with the natural bride preparing for her wedding day. The parable of the Bride of Christ and the natural bride is to mirror it against the natural to the spiritual so people will see the reflection of Christ in the wedding. When we look in the natural, as we prepare for our wedding day, we should see the parable or illustration of us preparing for our wedding day in the spiritual. In the natural, the bride sees her reflection as the bride in her mirror. In the spiritual room, when we look into our mirror, we should see the reflection of our Groom. Our mirror as the Bride of Christ should reflect Jesus.

To understand our divine insurance plan, we look at insurance in the natural. In the natural, insurance, i.e., home insurance, car insurance, etc., are types of insurance policies that are in place to give us a sense of false security and peace. But none of these policies can provide 100% coverage; there are stipulations, such as acts of God. In the spiritual realm, we have the divine insurance policy, Psalm 91. This plan is better than all the insurance policies men can provide. When we dwell in God's secret place and live in His presence, we have 100% coverage, protection, deliverance, and long, satisfying life in Him. We don't have to worry about a problem because the plan was paid in FULL over two thousand years ago. Everything we need is in His divine insurance policy. Again, the natural man doesn't comprehend this; he only sees in the natural.

The Bible says,

"But as it is written: "Eye has not seen, nor ear heard, Nor have entered into the heart of man The things which God has prepared for those who love Him," 1 Corinthians 2:9.

In the natural, the unborn baby is developed in the womb. In the spiritual realm, our prayers are in the womb of the earth, waiting to be birth. As we continue to pray, seeking God, He in return answers them according to His will and plan. When we allow our prayers to develop inside the womb, the Holy Spirit guides us in what to pray, so our prayers are effective, resulting in God's Kingdom and power manifesting upon the earth.

We cannot look at birth in the natural, without first seeing it in the spiritual realm. In the spiritual realm, when the baby (our prayer) is pushed out, the righteousness of God saturates the earth. Look at it this way: The Bride of Christ has to reflect Jesus, and the Divine Insurance Plan reflects what we have in Jesus, when we abide by the stipulation, resulting in our prayers (the unborn baby) being pushed out our womb, changing the atmosphere, bringing God's glory upon the earth.

The Reflection of Jesus, The Christ in Us

As Believers: What we look like is the Bride of Christ. What we receive is the Divine Insurance Plan. How it is conceived and manifested is through the womb of prayer. As a result: We Become Jesus' Reflection on the Earth.

When we realize who we are, whom we belong to, and the benefits, promises, and power we have, we could make a difference in the world. Jesus prayed for us to become one, as He, the Father, and the Holy Spirit are One.

"I do not pray for these alone, but also for those who [j]will believe in Me through their word; 21 that they all may be one, as You, Father, are in Me, and I in You; that they also may be one in Us, that the world may believe that You sent Me. 22 And the glory which You gave Me I have given them, that they may be one just as We are one: 23 I in them, and You in Me; that they may be made perfect in one, and that the world may know that You have sent Me, and have loved them as You have loved Me," John 17: 21-23.

Through His Holy Spirit, Jesus wants to empower us with His power, enabling us to tread on scorpions, healed the sick deliver the captives free, mend the brokenhearted, and declare that the Kingdom of God upon the earth. In our oneness, He wants to radiate His reflection of Who He is in us. We are to be His light on the earth, penetrating the forces of darkness, causing them to flee. In His power, we are to stand and portray our light as a beacon of hope for others to see and become saved. That is why we are still here on the earth, to reflect the image of Jesus. If it were not so, the moment we got saved, God would have called us home.

Now that we understand how God shows us in the natural, the things of God in the spiritual, it is time for the Believer, the

Body of Christ, to reflect His image upon the earth during this dispensation of time.

FOOTNOTES

1. https://en.wikipedia.org/wiki/Insurance, page 35.

2./3. https://enduringword.com/bible-commentary/psalm-91/, page 42

4. https://becomingchristians.com/2018/02/26/20-most-surprising-lessons-from-psalm-91-you-probably-never-heard of/, page 46.

5. https://boords.com/ethos-pathos-logos/what-is-kairos, page 70.

6. https://www.gotquestions.org/kairos-meaning.html, page 71.

Grace Black-Kimble

About the Author

Grace W. Black-Kimble, is a born-again Believer and a mighty Woman of God. She lives in Gadsden, Alabama, with her husband, Pastor Harold Kimble, of twenty years. She has one son, Dwayne L. Crowder, and one granddaughter, Kayla L. Crowder. She is an ordained, licensed minister. She received a Doctrinal of Theology-Honors Degree from Washington Saturday Bible College. She is a retired teacher from T. C. Williams High School ("Remember the Titans"), Alexandria, Virginia. She has taught, trained, and written many documents throughout her life, helping Believers know more about Jesus, making them better servants for His Kingdom.

CPSIA information can be obtained
at www.ICGtesting.com
Printed in the USA
LVHW081100071021
699805LV00006B/163